POISED® for Results

ENDORSEMENTS

Our senior leadership team has leveraged the POISED Model for several years. This book beautifully reinforced what we are doing while providing fresh new insights! POISED was a game-changer, providing a living strategic planning process alongside a consistent execution model—and yet is flexible enough to welcome unplanned strategic opportunities. Since implementing the POISED Model, we now enjoy an operational rhythm and a consistent cadence within our senior leadership meetings. Our senior leadership team is aligned and with alignment comes an enjoyment of our collective leadership journey. As a Christian institution of higher learning, no margin equates to no mission and the stakes are incredibly high. I highly recommend this book—and the "plug and play" POISED Model—for university and school leaders who need a sense of calm within this moment of great disruption.

-Dr. Daniel W. Johnson
President, Wisconsin Lutheran College

As the former VP of Engineering at General Mills, I had the opportunity to work with PaR systems and Mark Wrightsman for more than 15 years. I was always impressed with the alignment of priorities and strategies that extended up and down the organization at PaR. Equally impressive was how, over time, the team just kept getting better. As one responsible for a large global organization, I know how challenging it can be to align the many stakeholders responsible for success. I was always intrigued with both the financial success and the culture at PaR. Then I read *POISED® for Results* and now I know how they did it! Each of the building blocks rests on proven leadership principles—and this book brings them to life in a simple, organized way that will work for any organization. Kudos and thanks for assembling such an important tool that will ensure success for anyone who lives the process!

-Gregg Stedronsky
VP of Global Engineering, General Mills (retired)

POISED® for Results offers leaders the guidance they need to excel and produce results in an organization where everyone is engaged to the maximum level. Staying grounded as a leader on what is truly important is crucial for success. After serving in the U.S. Navy, I led IT, Quality and Security organizations at Medtronic when Bill George headed the organization. After I left Medtronic, I went to PaR Systems to work for Mark Wrightsman who I have known for more than 20 years. Mark's leadership and mentorship allowed me to gain the skills to start my own company supporting the Defense Industrial Base. For leadership practitioners, this book takes the best of Mark's learning and practical experience—from his executive career at GE working for Jack Welch to PaR systems where we helped build everything from spaceships to Teslas to the robotic crane system for Chernobyl. Dr. Scott Gostchock added to and elevated the POISED Model, and this book, through his deep experience as an educator and as a practitioner using the model to drive organizational leaders forward in a meaningful, positive, and consultative manner.

-Scott Singer
Captain, U.S. Navy (retired)
VP of Quality, IT, Security, PaR Systems (retired)
President and Founder, CyberNINES

In the Tech business world of software, security, Internet hardware, and the Cloud, we are used to moving fast, very efficiently and under hard growth metrics. We must be entrepreneurial. We need to be effective. *POISED® for Results* enables a team to gel, to work honestly, and to get to the point on everything important to a tech business—and to do it with agility! The POISED Model ensures key issues and opportunities are identified and acted upon. The model also ensures the Mission is ultra-important and drives people to work at their peak to accomplish the Vision. Most startups are understaffed, with people performing multiple roles and pushing the envelope. The tools in this book embed vision into the team and ensure people who are best fitted for new, challenging roles can embrace constant change in the thinly structured environments that enable them to be creative and rise to the top. *POISED® for Results* is for you if you are in Tech or any kind of organization and you want efficient, productive tools to guide it to operate at the highest effectiveness. I have known Mark and Dr. Scott for years—their experience and expertise has been poured into this POISED process and model and I highly recommend it to help your team achieve success!

-Jay W. Johnson
Partner, P2G Capital and Partner2Learn
VP/GM of Security Services, VeriSign
Co-Founder, SecureIT
VP of Sales, Air Defense & NTObjectives, Inc.
VP of Business Development, GE Technology Management Services
Founding Member, Unisys Network Enable
Board Member, Grace in Action

POISED® for Results shares decades of real-life experience that will help other organizations reach their full potential. *POISED® for Results* and its business model place a key foundational emphasis on People and integrate other critical areas required for organizational success. I've had the opportunity to practice leadership within growing organizations for 40 years. Having a business model was extremely advantageous—it aligned people to shared views and methods for how to approach their business. *POISED® for Results* identifies the areas needed for a successful business. I'm pleased the POISED Model starts with People, and I endorse each of the six elements, along with the guidance of how to apply it within your organization. The commitment to a business model starts with leadership of the organization and then permeates throughout the organization. Once your organization is aligned using the POISED Model, your team will experience significant advantages in operating your business. I encourage you to implement this system and am confident improved future results will reward your effort.

-Paul Holzhueter
VP of Business Development, Malt-O-Meal (retired)
Group VP, Hubbard Milling Company (retired)

Through more than 30 years of human resources experience, I have not seen many business models that reflect the crucial need of strategic human resource management or have incorporated it into the strategy discussion like in *POISED® for Results*. By implementing the POISED Model, you will have the ability to transform your business by ensuring that all employees are Aligned, Engaged, and have the right Fit for the organization. Organizations that do not have all three components are not likely to reach their full potential. I have seen first-hand how this Model has helped employees become more engaged in their work, thereby improving the performance of the company.

-Karen O'Rourke
VP of Human Resources, PaR Systems
Senior HR Consultant

Mark Wrightsman & Scott Gostchock, Ed.D.

POISED®
FOR
RESULTS

Amplify Your Strengths and
Lead Your Team and Organization
to Sustained, Elevated Performance

NEW YORK

LONDON • NASHVILLE • MELBOURNE • VANCOUVER

POISED® for Results

Amplify Your Strengths and Lead Your Team and Organization to Sustained, Elevated Performance

Published in New York, New York, by Morgan James Publishing. Morgan James is a trademark of Morgan James, LLC. www.MorganJamesPublishing.com

Proudly distributed by Ingram Publisher Services.

Morgan James BOGO™

A **FREE** ebook edition is available for you or a friend with the purchase of this print book.

CLEARLY SIGN YOUR NAME ABOVE

Instructions to claim your free ebook edition:
1. Visit MorganJamesBOGO.com
2. Sign your name CLEARLY in the space above
3. Complete the form and submit a photo of this entire page
4. You or your friend can download the ebook to your preferred device

ISBN 9781631959639 paperback
ISBN 9781631959646 ebook
Library of Congress Control Number:
2022937906

Cover & Interior Design by:
Christopher Kirk
www.GFSstudio.com

Morgan James PUBLISHING **Builds** *with...* **Habitat for Humanity®** Peninsula and Greater Williamsburg

Morgan James is a proud partner of Habitat for Humanity Peninsula and Greater Williamsburg. Partners in building since 2006.

Get involved today! Visit MorganJamesPublishing.com/giving-back

DEDICATION

*To all of those who have taken time and interest and invested
their personal energy into developing us and helping us grow
To all of you readers who have the desire to do the same now—
to help others grow and to develop
Giving thanks for the opportunity to use the talents and experiences
that each of us uniquely has been given
May the learnings painstakingly earned and carefully crafted
into* POISED® for Results *be of benefit to you, your teams,
and many others now and in the future*

AND TO OUR FAMILIES

*Thank you for supporting our commitment to make a difference
in others' lives as you make an inspiring, loving difference in ours*

TABLE OF CONTENTS

Discover the story of the authors' inspiration for writing the book. Learn about Excellence as a theme. Understand definitions of Model and Process to set the foundation for the POISED® for Results approach.

Explore the POISED process and the POISED Model's six key elements. See how the model serves as a Global Positioning System (GPS) for your organization's excellence journey.

Leverage Strengths-Based Leadership so People growth and development fuel the organization. Drive organizational success by emphasizing Mission-Vision-Values (MV^2), providing training, developing people to their fullest capability, and maximizing their strengths.

> *Infuse the People element with Octane to boost the organization's energy. Reinforce the power of Alignment-Engagement-Fit (AEF). Build results-driven Octane practices including AEF at all levels, continuous improvement and organizational learning, and optimal stress.*

> *Focus the organization by identifying priorities: intentional, key actions critical to success that address challenges, metrics, opportunities, and strategic imperatives. Enable wise use of resources and select key metrics with client, employee, and improvement urgency.*

> *Drive forward from MV². Scan strategic, operational, and competitive conditions to define critical thought leader inputs (Challenges and Opportunities). Transform long-range winning Strategy into short-term, actionable tasks while cascading and communicating at all levels.*

Develop and sustain a focus on high-margin services/products that generate financial value to propel organizational growth. Maintain a hyper-focus on client-facing and internal costs for optimal value creation. Measure what matters to guide leaders and to keep the organization on track.

Drive delivery of services/products with discipline and customer focus. Build a routine rhythm of reporting, analysis, and action that ensures efficient and effective work at all levels. Promote agility to adapt quickly, flexibly, and effectively to evolving market and customer needs.

Step up to the challenge and embrace the opportunity to lead your organization to new levels of performance. Commit to implement the systematic, proven POISED Model and fulfill your leadership purpose—now and into the future—to impact business results and people's lives.

AUTHORS' NOTE

"…disciplined people engaged in disciplined thought
and taking disciplined action create great organizations
that produce exceptional results."
–Jim Collins, Author, *Good to Great*–

Excellence at any level—self, team, organizational—is a hard-won accomplishment that challenges a leader's values, actions, decisions, thought processes and, quite frankly, optimism, resilience, and determination. Just a brush with excellence much less a foothold for sustained, elevated excellence requires steadfast commitment and poise to navigate ever-present changes in workplace, industry, and global conditions.

As the authors of *POISED® for Results* and designers of the "plug-and-play" POISED Model, Dr. Scott Gostchock and Mark Wrightsman have worked together for around two decades leading up to this publication. Dr. Scott brings a wealth of education and leadership training background while Mark has been an organizational performance practitioner for 45 years.

Together, we offer the POISED Model, practical tools, and our unique experiences in *POISED® for Results* with belief in and confidence that it will elevate your organization's performance.

OUR BIG WHY

As we were finalizing *POISED® for Results*, a long-time business friend and mutual mentor, Gregg Stedronsky, challenged me (Mark) to explain the book's "why". Gregg has significant global experience, process expertise, and regularly has compelling insights into all aspects of a well-run organization, especially people.

His question to me was: *What gave you the burning desire to spend several years articulating the POISED organizational leadership model in this book?*

A desire for articulating the model and process for organizational excellence, and developing associated tools, to activate others is driven from my strengths—which start with learning and organizing, as well as a core belief that there is always a better way—as long as that way begins with basic principles and relies fully on people and process. My journey has been exciting, rewarding, challenging, global, and filled with intense learning to the extent I have felt compelled to capture these learnings for others to derive benefit—one significant purpose Dr. Scott and I feel compelled to pursue in our lives.

Early in my career, I had an opportunity to work for General Electric (GE) during famed CEO Jack Welch's era. As you might expect, this opportunity was filled with intensity and learning. Some experienced this time as high stress; others saw it as incredibly energizing to work in a super-competitive environment with extremely strong colleagues around the world, led by a CEO intent on making GE the best company in the world. Later in the opportunities presented to me, whether leading in a rapidly changing robotics industry with four very different Boards of Directors over 20 years, the hard-nosed automotive tech world, or the global Unisys information systems market, I experienced many high-stress situations and that taught me about positioning for elevated performance, whether through positive or painful means. Most importantly, I learned through experience with many excellent leaders, as well as countless tough situations, the importance of leadership principles and processes.

My experience cultivated a strong personal desire to share my learnings in the hope that others will receive benefit and perhaps more readily overcome or avoid similar issues, while achieving sustained, elevated team performance. One experience in Japan in the early 1990s is seared into my memory and taught me enduring lessons—and may provide you, the reader, a peek into an example of my desire to share this information to activate you.

GE relocated me and my family from our base in Singapore to Japan, bringing my combined nuclear and power systems/turbine generators background and success in building aftermarket teams. For years, clients like Tokyo Electric Power demanded that GE provide aftermarket support for the billions of dollars they invested in new GE power plants for Japan; this was all to provide Japanese clients a competitive alternative to Toshiba and Hitachi. Jack Welch insisted someone lead this effort and I was chosen to follow-through on Jack's commitment to clients. At just 35 years old, I was far too young to be a senior leader in Japan except that in Welch's GE, the Japanese had begun to begrudgingly accept some very young leaders GE had chosen.

I arrived in Tokyo and we set up office, re-tooled the position descriptions of several incumbent engineers and service team members, and began hiring local Japanese talent. Just as we were getting started, a high-profile client maintenance issue surfaced at an aging nuclear plant. This maintenance steam leak, a relatively minor steam turbine issue, became a high-profile dilemma under the magnifying glass of the Japanese Quality mandate. As a result, the plant was shut down, creating a high-profile problem that made the local news and put pressure on the utility client's upper management.

A minor maintenance issue became a major crisis and the utility urgently sought solutions. GE's U.S. maintenance group mentioned we had a one-day robotic solution to smoothly grind the turbine flange and rapidly eliminate the leak. While our Japan team was just learning about and discussing the solution, the client jumped at the "magic GE robotic solution". Within days, we had a large purchase order and were mobilizing resources from the U.S. and Japan. The team assembled and went to work. The local newspaper even reported that the power plant would be *saved* by the high-tech GE solution!

During weeks of trial and error to get the magic robotic solution to fulfill its promise, huge difficulties arose and continued. Our team put in long hours, working 7 days a week. Despite a large territory, I spent considerable time at this particular site. The pressure kept increasing. The press was actively reporting the GE challenges at the plant. Utility client management pressure grew more and more intense. It also seemed as though the entrenched Japanese competitor who controlled the overall site maintenance activities was working against us at every turn.

After weeks and significant client and GE management pressure to do anything and everything to succeed, I was summoned back to the plant site, arriving by train late on a Thursday evening to check into a tiny Japanese hotel room near the plant. Just as I was checking in near midnight, the Plant Manager delivered a surprise message to me: *be onsite for a 1 a.m. meeting.* I traveled the remaining miles by car, met up with our team, and then walked into a site leadership meeting filled with Japanese utility and competitor leaders ready to grill the GE team intensely, and especially the senior (35-year-old) leader, me.

Following grueling discussions about the highly technical and quality procedure- and process-driven issues, we concluded the meetings and I walked over in the early hours of Friday to meet with the full GE team, U.S. and Japanese employees working together, sweating together, without much sleep over the past many weeks. We intensely discussed the problems, brainstormed actions, and worked through the night. By the time I left to return to Tokyo on Friday evening, having been awake for the past 2 days, an ominous sense of failure hung in the air among our team members. The momentously chest-tightening series of weeks culminated in GE being removed from the project a few days after the 2-day ordeal at the site.

In Japan, failure was not acceptable or acknowledged. Some were fearful in this environment; "suicide by train" was an occasional response by Japanese workers to a bad situation. And, this GE failure felt very bad. As our team re-grouped following the client rejection, we discussed lessons learned. We were thankful the response was mature and no one seemed threatened as we calmly talked about the learnings.

First, we dug into robotics. Yes, GE had done the robotic machining in the U.S., *so why didn't it work at this Japanese nuclear power plant?* As it turns out, with just a bit more digging, we learned that GE (a) NEVER performed similar robotic work at a nuclear plant, not even in the U.S. and (b) NEVER had this particular robotic machining team experienced the rigors of working under Japanese Quality processes at nuclear plants. This situation was compounded by the new formation of a Japanese and American team I was charged with developing; we all were learning new roles as we learned about each other and the merged cultural requirements. We were all committed to improve but dreaded the thought of a long, arduous rebuilding of a Japanese client's trust when we had flat-out failed.

I had a lot to think about that Friday night as I took the train back to Tokyo, and just to help imprint an indelible memory, an earthquake that hit nearby Kobe just happened to kill the power in my last subway. We sat in the dark, motionless for what seemed like an eternity. After the subway re-started and I arrived at my stop, I walked home from the station. There, I found my wife and children awake as she readied them for earthquake emergency evacuation from our 17th story apartment. While things had just calmed down and an evacuation was not required, we did not sleep much that night. I was trying to function through more than 48 hours without sleep.

What happened next was amazing. Within a few days of the failure, the utility client in Japan began inviting us to talk about the many other projects that had lined up. Within a short period of time, we were given a series of orders, all for services and equipment that were our bread-and-butter where we could excel. And, we were given every chance to succeed over time.

Why? My Japanese mentor, Chuck Miyamoto (with whom I learned to collaborate closely and from whom I would seek advice for any important decision in Japan), and client-facing GE leaders JT and Fukuda-san, explained it to me; while we failed, the client admitted they pulled GE in as a magic solution without much selling from GE. They too, in an uncommon Japanese manner, missed many important questions and process steps. Most importantly, while they knew the GE Japanese workers always worked hard, they had never seen Americans (including their leaders) work so hard, never giving up. We had made a deep positive impression in the midst of a deep failure.

People, process, priorities, strategy and strategic execution, and *EVERYTHING WE DID*, were identified as important to our rebuilding and our lessons learned. We reset strategy, reidentified priorities, refocused our team, recommitted to processes of client communication and ensuring proposals were vetted, and reinforced other aspects required to reset the new business. Within 18 months, the business grew significantly, a high-tech joint venture effort launched, and some years later my Japanese successor was able to report growing this startup business from that initial foundation to more than $200 million in annual revenue. The seeds of failure germinated success and launched my career-long commitment to the elements that became the POISED Model.

Let me also share briefly "why Dr. Scott AND Mark" ended up writing about and coaching leadership together. Several decades ago, I (Mark) first had a chance to observe Dr. Scott teaching middle school students, treating them like adults, emphasizing their strengths, and modeling team behavior. His young students walked away motivated to improve the lives of others around them. I was blown away.

Over the years, I have seen Dr. Scott's amazing ability to teach, motivate, and guide individuals and teams with all levels of experience to elevated performance. His ability to relate, coach leadership concepts, and inspire a can-do positive approach to life and organizational problems is at the highest level. Dr. Scott seeks partners and, as a true servant-leader, moves through open doors to create opportunities—opportunities for others.

I believe you will understand as the POISED Model unfolds in this book why we felt compelled to share it widely. My learnings from Japan, numerous other gut-wrenching circumstances we overcame, and the hard-won rewarding times reinforced how people supported by organizational leadership principles and processes produce results and elevated performance.

OUR WRITING APPROACH

In writing this organizational leadership book, we leverage actual experience and knowledge resulting from the gift of working with many others. We share our experiences and anticipate that you will relate to your own experiences and add insights from your own situation while exploring and, hopefully, implementing lessons and learnings imparted in *POISED® for Results*.

We chose to co-write this book intentionally, weaving together the experiences from both our primary realms—educational expertise and leadership training—and from real-life under-fire leadership. We readily admit that we have moved fast enough and long enough to have made as many mistakes as anyone! We also both lay claim to the title of "life-long learner", willingly and readily, and sometimes just eventually, eager to learn from our mistakes and through experiences as part of good teams and of teams with enormous challenges.

As we write, we include a note on which author, Dr. Scott or Mark, leads the narrative or offers the example whenever such identification provides relevance. As well, you will notice we may use different and unique styles as authors and we made an intentional decision not to merge these two distinct styles. This enables us to share information and thinking from both of our backgrounds with an authentic voice that suits our experiences. We hope you find this approach beneficial and perhaps even a bit more interesting than the typical leadership book.

We reference POISED as both a *model* and a *process*. As teams progress through learning about and using POISED, we have been asked: *Can it be both?* and *What's the difference?*

So, let us start out with some background and simple definitions in every-day language. Going to the online *Dictionary.com* explains why it can be both a model and a process:

Model—"a system or thing used as an example to follow or imitate"

Process—"a series of actions or steps taken in order to achieve a particular end"

Therefore, we designed and share the POISED Model as a proven "plug and play" framework to follow for accomplishing results . . . and achieving sustained, elevated performance. This book explains each component of the simplified model. While the model is straightforward, with six key elements depicted visually and quite simply, we offer detailed information of each step with a goal to provide you the understanding and motivation to get started in following the model to achieve amazing results.

And, we promote the steps and actions in the POISED Model as a systematic (repeatable, disciplined) process. Following the process, users build on the foundation of the ***People*** and ***Octane*** elements, focus on priorities ***Identified*** with key metrics, synthesize the priorities into a comprehensive and compelling ***Strategy*** that engages the organization, ensure the ***Engine of Profitability*** receives continual attention, and execute the plan in a disciplined way through what leaders in the organization ***Do***. We also share tools (in an Appendix) that are a part of the POISED process and help leaders achieve their desired results in the most efficient (rapid) and effective (optimal) way.

Following the clear model and using the step-by-step process accelerate performance as the team aligns around POISED and leads to results . . . and sustained, elevated performance. Toward this goal, we encourage each reader to visualize clearly how to grow his/her own role as a leader and how he/she develops other leaders along the journey to produce results and elevate the overall organization.

As we spoke to collaborators, often they recommended we speak up-front to who our intended audience is likely to be. Leaders arrive to their roles with precious little instruction or support in the crucible of leading others and their organizations. We expect that a diversity of leaders, from front-line to executive and from early to late career, will benefit significantly from reading our organizational leadership book and applying the practical model.

First, seasoned leaders may recognize many of the principles in this book yet also find that the accessible and repeatable POISED Model helps them successfully apply a broad range of their learning into a workable, results-driven approach.

Second, we also chose to pose the lessons in this book in a manner so newer (and future) leaders may learn this organizational leadership approach without the clutter of hard-to-understand terms and concepts.

Because some leaders may want to dig deeper than is typical in a book, we have endeavored to explain (in greater detail than a handbook) and to provide diagrams of our process and tools for easy application and use. Finally, because we have designed within and applied this model across large, medium, and small businesses— and in education and ministry environments as well—you will find direct applicability as a leader in *any* type of organization.

Throughout, our purpose is to share a holistic organizational leadership model we believe will help make your role as a leader in any situation rewarding—for you and especially for all the leaders you are striving to create. By definition, our proven model helps you and your teams be POISED for results and sustained, elevated performance.

We understand that being an organizational leader is a tough job, sort of like being a fighter jet pilot, freighter captain, orchestra conductor, sports team coach, and foster parent all wrapped into one. And we know from direct experience that learning and using a disciplined leadership and management approach seems complicated. Yet, consider how your current daily, monthly, quarterly, and annual priorities surface now—and how you battle every day to find the time, resources, skills, and energy to get ahead of the curve.

Business people have grown accustomed to "fighting fires" and utter sayings like "culture eats strategy for breakfast" and "no plan survives contact with the enemy" as rationale to curb investment in culture creation, strategy development, and planning. In the end, performance excellence guru Peter Drucker's thinking sets the tone for your organizational role as a leader: *managers do things right and leaders do the right things. POISED® for Results* offers a guide to identify the right things (leadership) and then do them right (management).

As a leader, you have a choice: stick with the status quo or stretch your organization to reach new levels of sustained, elevated performance. We hope you learn and enjoy your journey studying and applying POISED. Remember, leadership is a *contact* support . . . and no waiting period is required. Make the choice to reach sustained, elevated performance your team, customers, and stakeholders deserve.

LET'S GO!

INTRODUCTION

"It would be better if everyone worked together
as a system, with the aim for everyone to win."
–W. Edwards Deming, Renowned Management Consultant–

The Global Positioning System (GPS) has revolutionized travel for almost every person in our modern world. Just think about it for a minute. When you used to go from one location to another, how did you get there? Did you ever try to go somewhere without directions and clearly laid out plans? If you did, it probably did not work too well. You took wrong turns, got lost, maybe even stopped to ask for directions when you became frustrated. In the end, seeking a destination without directions did not work well . . . or even at all.

We became accustomed to the use of hard-copy maps, written directions, dictated directions, landmarks, memory, and so many other ways to get from one destination to the next. These all worked with different degrees of success (did you ever try to re-fold a map?). These methods all were certainly better than no directions at all, but they could be a lot of work and cumbersome for limited results, accuracy, and almost no ability to change.

Then, the Sputnik era and U.S. Navy navigational tracking in the 1950s ushered in GPS technology and it all got so much easier. Through different means suddenly we had access to clear, succinct, and accurate directions with on-the-spot ability to flex and to adjust as needed to get to our final goal or destination. Today we travel with ease of mind knowing how to get from one place to the next. GPS revolutionized travel for us all and led to greater success in reaching our destination in the fastest and most effective way possible.

GPS is certainly vital for each of us. We need it to get where we want to go. The same is true for our company, organization, team, and even our family: we need a GPS to ensure we know where we are starting (a baseline) and where we need and hope to go (an objective).

Is there such a thing as a GPS for the people and teams in our businesses and lives? How would we use such a GPS to guide us? The POISED Model is this GPS. The POISED process—when fully utilized—helps guide and lead us to where we want and need to go.

THE POISED PROCESS

What is the POISED process? And how will it help my organization get from where we are to where we need to be?

Simply, the POISED process represents a clear and holistic way to approach organizational leadership, emphasizing targeted strategic planning and follow-on elements key to performance. The process leads to an overarching plan, through an assessment and leadership guide from the present to the very bright future you desire to create.

Now, how does the POISED process work?

The POISED process, like a GPS, relies on a clear roadmap of foundational milestones and markers:

- **Starting point.** Where is my company/organization right now? What is the baseline from which we must move forward? Once you have conducted this guided assessment, you have established the baseline and begun to implement the POISED process.

- **Aims and objectives.** After entering the process with this starting data, you then begin to input the directions (your objectives). These next steps include specifying where we want our organization to be long-term (vision) and, if we are going to be there in the future, what first steps (actions) we need to take. This is just like using the GPS in our car or on our phone: we decide where we want to go, identify where we are starting, and then choose a navigational pathway with the first turns we will take to get us moving and tracking to our destination.

- **Strategic roadmap.** Following the first two steps that provide a strategic *framework* for a desired future, leaders then walk through the key POISED leadership elements to generate a strategic *roadmap* for actions aligned with the framework. The roadmap specifies the actions and resources (human and financial) required to reach our destination.

- **Performance monitoring and adjustment.** When we drive our vehicles and navigate using our car or phone GPS, we check in and make adjustments frequently based on traffic, street closures, accidents, etc. Teams and organizations must establish interim goals, in-process deadlines and indicators, and measurable targets, then take the pulse of performance to evaluate progress and adjust accordingly. Driving with our eyes closed is a bad choice!

The POISED Model operates just like a GPS, giving us data and knowledge we need to make adjustments that keep our journey on track. A GPS gives you real-time guidance such as "make a U-turn now", "keep left in 500 feet", or "recalculating." A GPS adjusts navigation in relation to situations and changes in the environment to enable necessary adjustments that keep you on track to reach your final destination. The POISED Model does the same.

POISED represents a living process and plan that allow you and your organization to be agile. You may make changes in your plan in real time "while you drive" to better meet the challenges and opportunities that present themselves—and as rapidly as you can acknowledge the human missteps that people invariably make. POISED presents carefully developed resources to help you and your organization become creative, innovative, learning, and nimble to maximize opportunities as they arise and reroute/pivot as needed to stay on track . . . or even to get ahead. You can "recalculate" and make the "U-turn" right away to not get lost, lose momentum and, ultimately, lose out.

As you begin to dig into this book and the POISED process, you will learn how important it is to have a starting point and a clear destination. You will also learn the required steps to navigate your journey successfully and to continue moving forward no matter what detours may come your way. These steps take diligence, but the effort that requires is nothing compared to the resource burn, human churn, and complexity invited by typical organizations when they choose NOT to apply a holistic approach to performance.

Leaders arrive in their roles with little instruction to drive performance. Yet, there IS a way to lead organizations that produces results and sustained, elevated performance. The POISED Model and process integrate centuries of business leadership experience and recent, real-life expertise. The model assembles an approach that targets and defines a way for organizations to excel. The process involves a holistic integration of people—the fuel of an organization—along with the engine of strategy, finances, and other pivotal components to accomplish success for any organization of any size or type.

THE POISED KEY ELEMENTS

The POISED Model (depicted visually below) integrates six elements key (most important) to organizational success and sustained, elevated performance:

- **People**—the fuel of every organization; the true lifeblood and foundation of any successful organization, emphasizing developing and engaging people and Alignment-Engagement-Fit (AEF) for each person involved
- **Octane**—the additives that boost the fuel (people) of the organization; an organization's highest-level leaders, Strengths-based approach, continual improvement, and other enabling resources and methods
- **Identify**—the most important measurements, strategies, and priorities identified and then tracked in a clear and concise manner, helping the organization clearly see and address challenges and opportunities and Drive Business Solutions (DBS) toward success
- **Strategy**—the overarching plan that incorporates all aspects of the POISED Model clearly and simply, articulating a winning strategy for chosen market(s) and product(s) or service(s) based on the strengths of the organization, and setting measurable in-process and stretch goals focused on success for everyone

- **<u>Engine</u> of <u>P</u>rofitability (EoP)**—the focus on critical financial elements vital for sustainability, enabling durable performance by keeping sight on fueling profits to invest in growth and fund the success of the organization
- **<u>D</u>o**—the operational rhythm of thoughtful daily, weekly, monthly, quarterly, and annual actions by the whole team focused on elevating the complete organization, focusing on Mission, Vision, and Values (MV²) as the driving force for the entire enterprise, and ensuring optimal implementation of the POISED process

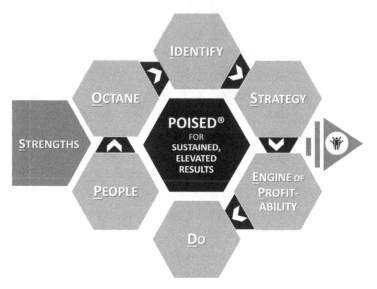

What's next? Where do we go from here? In Chapter 1, we start unpacking the POISED process starting with the "P" of the POISED Model—People—the fuel of and foundation for any successful organization. The journey begins now to take you to your destination, poised for success through the POISED process, your organization's GPS.

1

PEOPLE

"The essential difference in service is not machines or 'things.'
The essential difference is minds, hearts, spirits, and souls."
–Herb Kelleher, Southwest Airlines CEO–

Leadership . . . **what does this term and concept** *really* **mean?** In our work with clients, we teach leadership and start by defining it as *the ability to serve others and to assist them to reach their fullest potential.* As leaders pursue this human-value emphasis, a productivity chain-reaction occurs: leaders invest in serving and developing their team members, organizational productivity increases, and the organization maximizes today's opportunities, enabling the organization to meet and surpass future goals and objectives.

So how do leaders take the necessary actions to develop People and make this happen? Let us begin with a story.

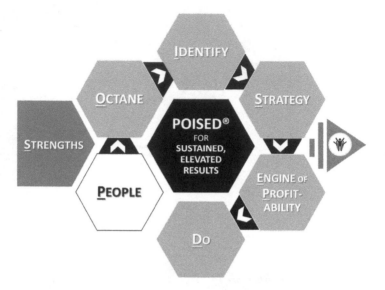

LEADERSHIP STORY

Early in my professional life, I (Dr. Scott) worked in the fast-food industry. I started as a grill person. Then, I received training in every other facet of the operation, leading me to become a salaried manager. My future was mapped out in front of me with the corporation. It was a terrific opportunity.

Why was I selected to be a manager with future growth options mapped out in front of me? Well, I placed my focus consistently on the people. I gained experience in every position on the team. I knew what every person went through and I could relate to them. I took this knowledge and relatability and then leveraged it to make others great in any way I possibly could. In so doing, others noticed me. Leadership noticed me. Corporate noticed me. I was not striving to "be noticed", but the natural outcome of focusing on serving others, recognizing and optimizing their strengths, and putting it all together to enable a high-performing team gets noticed quickly. True leadership starts and ends with *people*.

People and teams are vital for the success of every great organization and the critical focus of progressive leadership. As we move into the first component of POISED—People—you will see clearly why this element is foundational for all other facets of POISED and future success of the organization.

The people on any team and within any organization are the lifeblood for success. The stronger the people and the more positive and growth-centered their leaders' approach to people, the greater likelihood that people will meet and exceed their goals. *So, how do you ensure this productivity chain reaction?* Start with understanding and building on the strengths of the people.

BUILDING ON STRENGTHS

Every person possesses unique talents and a strong, positive organizational culture relies on the diversity of strengths from all team members. Each person has different strengths the team needs to meet its mission successfully. *How do you figure these strengths out? How do you know what strengths people are bringing to the team?*

We have found the best way to answer these questions: using the resource of CliftonStrengths[1]. Our firm, Partner2Learn, employs a unique approach with CliftonStrengths to assist teams to discover each team members' Top 8 Strengths, to understand how those strengths work for the individual, and then to highlight how they work within a system of eight categories created by Jim Louwsma and Dr. Mark McCloskey (see Appendix) by leveraging unique strengths combinations and partner-up opportunities on the team.

This positive, strengths-first approach identifies the unique value of every team member, uncovers their needs so others may support them, helps the team increase productivity, and sets the stage for tremendous growth and overall success. To create a truly great culture and foundation for success with your people, you must strengthen your strengths, find your partner-up opportunities, and use your strengths for the benefit of others.

> To create a truly great culture and foundation for success with your people. you must strengthen your strengths, find your partner-up opportunities, and use your strengths for the benefit of others.

This strengths-based approach will help every team member to see each other for who they are gifted to be, rather than a deficiency view of who they are not or who they think they should be. By leveraging team member strengths, the team will drive higher engagement and overall productivity—leading to greater successes with less energy exerted. Success begins by starting with positive attributes, valuing each person's strengths, learning how they all work together, and building "positive vulnerability" to build a high level of trust and understanding

A team strengths-oriented approach to your people keeps everyone focused on the realities needed to accomplish organizational goals. Not only do you want the right people in the right seats on the bus[2], but you want the people in leadership roles holistically integrating all the POISED elements to fuel the organization through all operational facets. People are the key—they are the conduits for true success.

No business succeeds and then excels without highly qualified and committed people doing the right things based on their strengths. You must have such people in every role, from senior leadership to sales to reception and beyond. They also must serve in each functional area, including Finance, IT, HR, and each Sales and Delivery function.

No one person or role is more or less important to mission success. Everyone must fulfill their responsibilities at their highest capability level to realize true organizational success. When the organization recognizes that people are the lifeblood for its ultimate success, it must invest to develop people, exercise patience and persistence in personnel decisions, and ensure the right people fulfill the proper roles. This all starts with the leadership team.

LEADING TO TRANSFORM

Later in this book we will emphasize designing a POISED Strategic HR process focused on developing people and the organization continually. You guessed it . . . that transformative process also starts with the senior leadership team and encompasses the entire organization.

The leadership team must commit to the development of every person and actively live the values of the organization. Having interest in people is not enough. You have probably heard the "bacon and eggs" comparison to leadership; in a bacon and eggs breakfast, the chicken is interested, but the pig is committed. Do not be a chicken!

What are some steps to make sure you are developing your people? The below activities embody a process framework you can use in any organization.

1. Start with Strengths (see Appendix)
   - Each person is unique.
   - When people work from their strengths, they achieve more with less energy and become truly proficient in their positions.
   - When people work from their strengths, they are engaged and will push the business forward as they become brand ambassadors who live the mission, vision, and values.

- Use the strengths to properly place and/or train people and form teams; utilize Partner-Up Opportunities—Strengths for Others (SFO).

  Partner-up Opportunities are a unique way to look at your people to optimize efficiency and productivity. Encourage your people to strengthen their strengths and partner-up with others with different strengths to maximize energy and output and maximize engagement.

- Prioritize proper onboarding for new employees, not only to understand their strengths and their needs from others, but to orient them effectively to the business. Also, an honest assessment of people is essential; we use the Alignment-Engagement- Fit (AEF) tool (see Appendix), incorporating feedback from other leaders, as a foundational approach to this honest assessment.

  Alignment-Engagement-Fit (AEF)

  Alignment

  - Fully recognize, believe in, and carry out the organization's mission
  - Understand and unequivocally practice the organization's values
  - Realize and embody the vision of the organization
  - Embrace and move forward with clearly stated goals and success metrics

  Engagement

  - Be fully present and involved in organizational activities and responsibilities
  - Contribute actively to organizational improvement and overall quality

- Exercise accountability to self and others for organizational success
- Live values inside and outside of the organization—community matters

Fit

- Ensure right skills for position and duties, and ability to learn and use such skills, needed to achieve excellence
- Utilize strengths fully in position and completes duties for the good of the organization—using those strengths for others
- Recognize and capitalize on partner-up opportunities with others' strengths to maximize organizational productivity and success
- Improve strengths continually, as well as missional (mission and values alignment), emotional, and physical resiliency and health

All three AEF components are vitally important for all organizations. Alignment and Engagement are an absolute must. If either component is missing or not firing on all cylinders, the person involved cannot be productive. If Fit is the only issue, due to training needs or other professional development, the organization must consider how much time, energy, and resources can be devoted to the individual(s) to assist them to become the right Fit.

2. Establish a true understanding of Mission, Vision, and Values (MV^2)
   - To achieve true AEF, MV^2 must be clear and must be led and lived by the leadership

- If this component is lacking, an organization cannot achieve true success
- If this component is lacking, fix it!

3. Train!
   - Provide continual skills training and process orientation
     - Use your Developer strength people to help guide learning and to provide introductory training
     - Solid base-level training will result in success in each element of POISED in every role and will enable discovery of future high-level leaders to groom the next generation for success now and into the future
     - Know your people and their desires for growth
     - Help them to grow
     - Groom them to advance
     - This maximizes longevity of personnel, loyalty, and commitment; decreases voluntary turnover rate; and builds higher profits for all (among many other positive outcomes)
   - Develop and implement leadership training and cross-functional experience within a holistic approach to the training process
     - Keeps leaders longer in the company
     - Strengthens leaders for overall production and service for others
     - Ensures a learning environment for all through peer accountability, training, partnerships, and coaching for continuous improvement (CI)

- Encourages your people to know they are valuable, they will learn, and they will grow

4. Make tough personnel decisions driven by values, capability, and results, with compassion and respect, but without delay when it is time ("any decision is better than no decision") balancing:

   - Avoid excessive change that may damage an organization more than leaving less than fully capable people in place a bit longer
   - Accept that "an empty position is better than a person in the wrong position"
   - Take time, use the AEF resource, and make sure you have the right people; selecting anyone for the sake of having someone will cost more than taking time to find the "correct someone"
   - Undertake these actions in light of AEF, MV^2, and what will best serve the entire team and organization for true success

5. Drive Strategy (Chapter 4) and Engine of Profitability (Chapter 5) priorities, with all key leaders championing their respective priorities

6. Have a positive and proactive Strategic Human Resource Management Plan (Strategic HR Plan) and process in place for leaders to help people be truly productive while producing overall organizational results (In Chapter 2, Octane, and Chapter 6, Do, you will find more discussion of this Strategic HR Plan and the process. A Strategic HR Plan development process is found in highly effective organizations with a passion to develop their people. The POISED process infuses a Strategic HR Plan with additional octane for rapidly developing an organization's capability and effectiveness.)

A Strategic HR Plan development process is found in highly effective organizations with a passion to develop their people.

What framework will work well for a high-performing, strengths-based team and organization? Essential to a good team that produces results are these attributes[3]:

- Lead with a foundation of trust, emphasizing vulnerability-based trust (the ability to be wrong in a supported and encouraging environment) and positive conflict (always about MV^2 and Issues + Ideas [I^2])
- Build true commitment to the organization, the team, and others; say what you are going to do and then do what you say you are going to do
- Understand and support true accountability, the highest form of praise; when you hold someone accountable, you are saying they are important and what they are doing is important—if you do not hold someone accountable, you basically dismiss the person's value in who they are and in what they are doing
- Sustain an ultimate focus on *team* results—not what *I* do, but what *we* do for the success of the team and the organization

These foundational People elements, built from and designed to enhance individual and collective strengths, will help to ensure a high-performing team that will meet and exceed the organization's objectives.

People, the first and foundational component of POISED, are vital to the success of every organization. The better the fit of

the People, their strengths, their training, and the overall structure and culture of your team, the more success your organization may achieve. Invest resources, spend time on, and focus on
each People facet of the POISED Model and reap the results of
success.

As you grow your team and commit to develop and to serve
every individual, we encourage you to continue expanding your
own knowledge and skill in helping others grow. Life-long learning
is an essential aspect of organizational leadership. Dee Ann Turner's
Bet on Talent is one resource for continuing your own growth as a
leader focused on developing others[4]. We reference her book and
many other suggested resources in the Suggested Reading section at
the end of *POISED® for Results*.

Understanding then developing People will move
anyone forward in their professional life. What accel-
erates most careers, including our own, is engaging
people appropriately based on their strengths and
those of the team in which they serve. As you recognize
the strengths of your people, fully train and engage
them, and help them to see how amazing they are,
you will realize greater growth for your people and
momentum for the organization's overall success.

Octane—the fuel additive to drive forward momentum for
People—follows in Chapter 2.

POISED® Key Points Summary	
People	Develop each person to their fullest capability and enable optimal utilization of their Strengths
Octane	
Identify	
Strategy	
Engine of Profitability	
Do	
POISED® Integrated Model	

2

OCTANE

"Man is so made that when anything fires his soul,
impossibilities vanish."
–Jean de La Fontaine, French Poet–

Reaching a high-performance threshold feels like a miracle. Yet, every "miracle" of achieving a pinnacle of success—whether individual, team, or organizational—takes a disciplined approach and focused effort. It takes a boost to charge teams and individuals with the energy and enthusiasm to unleash their talents to create value for the organization.

The elements that produce this boost include alignment to purpose, productive "conflict", and an improvement focus. The POISED Model calls the approach and effort to create this boost Octane, a high-performance additive to the fuel (People) that drives success.

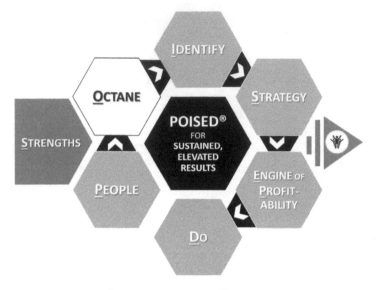

LEADERSHIP STORY

"The Miracle on Ice" at Lake Placid, New York, in 1980—when the U.S. Olympic hockey team defeated the "unbeatable" Soviet Union Olympic hockey team who had won four gold medals in a row dating back to 1964—offers an inspiring, compelling example of the proper use of Octane[5]. *Why?*

To prepare the all-amateur, collegiate-level U.S. team to face the mighty, seasoned, and professional Soviets, the coaches and players had to develop and demonstrate:

- True Alignment-Engagement-Fit (AEF) with the Mission, Vision, and Values (MV^2) of their country embedded into their team dynamics
- Focused ability to Drive Business Solutions (DBS), a process to discover true issues and then resolve them as a team to grow together for the good of each team member

- Amazing commitment to Continuous Improvement (CI), a mentality and manifestation of efforts to learn and to grow in all facets, in every way, every day

These elements set the foundation for Octane. Every team must have high Octane to reach its highest level and to accomplish the most for the whole team. According to 1980 U.S. Olympic Hockey Coach Herb Brooks, "I wanted people with a sound value system as you cannot buy values. You're only as good as your values. I learned early on that you do not put greatness into people. . .but somehow try to pull it out." The 1980 team was selected and then developed with Octane—and produced The Miracle on Ice, beating the daunting Russians and capturing the Gold Medal.

Are you ready for your miracle? Are you ready to do great things? Octane will fuel your way. Keep the Olympics Motto *Citius-Altius-Fortius* in mind: Swifter-Higher-Stronger!

ALIGNMENT-ENGAGEMENT-FIT

The POISED approach starts with proper and true AEF for People detailed in Chapter 1. Recognizing that people come to work every day to fulfill a mission they are passionate about, and aligning priorities and behaviors around the MV^2 daily, motivates top performance for the organization. Every person in the organization needs to be Aligned, Engaged, and the right Fit. If any of these three areas are missing or lacking, less than positive results will occur. When all three areas are fully in place for every individual, the organization's engine fires on all cylinders and the Octane-fed boost in results for the team will be clear and compelling.

What is true *Alignment*? As a leader, you must honestly evaluate and understand better if Alignment exists for each employee:

- Fully recognize, believe in, and carry out the organization's mission
- Understand and unequivocally accept the organization's values
- Realize and embody the vision of the organization
- Embrace and move forward with clearly stated goals and success metrics

What is true *Engagement*? Again, leaders must honestly evaluate and understand better if Engagement exists for each employee:

- Being fully present and involved in organizational activities and responsibilities
- Contributing actively to organizational improvement and overall quality
- Demonstrating accountability to self and others for organizational success
- Living organizational values inside and outside of the organization

What is true *Fit*? Finally, leaders must honestly evaluate and understand better if Engagement exists for each employee:

- Ensuring right skills for position and duties, or ability to learn and use such skills, needed to achieve excellence
- Leveraging strengths fully in the position and help employee to complete duties for the good of the organization, using those strengths for others
- Recognizing and capitalizing on partner-up opportunities with others' strengths to maximize organizational productivity and success

- Improving strengths continually, as well as possessing missional (mission and values alignment), emotional, and physical resiliency and health

All AEF components are vitally important for every organization. Alignment and Engagement are an absolute must. If either component is missing or is not firing on all cylinders, the person involved will not be productive. If Fit is the only issue due to training needs or other professional development gaps, the organization must devote time, energy, and resources to the individual(s) to assist them to become the right Fit.

Remember, true AEF centers on the following formula:

$$MV^2 + I^2 \text{ (Mission, Vision, Values + Issues and Ideas)}$$

The workplace culture and environment must build commitment to MV^2 and team members must be able to share openly and engage in positive discussion and debate (positive conflict) around I^2 to achieve optimal productivity. To help lead to this productivity, each organization must enable a practice of healthy and positive conflict. Driving Business Solutions (DBS) provides a disciplined structure to accomplish positive conflict and incorporates the individual strengths of each person on the team.

DRIVING BUSINESS SOLUTIONS

The need for positive conflict and the value of DBS stems from reality. Every organization deals with real issues, challenges, and obstacles. An organization prepared to deal openly, constructively, and efficiently with real-life issues can be far more effective in its performance and provide a much healthier environment for all team members.

The DBS process starts with a mentality built not around fear of or avoidance of problems, but around the team's dedication to find solutions to challenges. The DBS process has three key elements:

1. **Clarify**: Be clear on the issue. Give all team members the opportunity to reflect and to give input, especially individuals with CliftonStrengths' Problem Identification Strengths (Strategic, Ideation, Intellection) and those closest to the issue.

2. **Gather Team Inputs**: Discuss important aspects related to the issue. Always keep aligned on MV^2, identify ideas to help create understanding, and drive toward resolution of the clarified issue.

3. **Find a Way Forward**: Facilitate the team action plan development, specifying owner(s) and timeline (who does what by when). Ensure all team members provide input, especially individuals with CliftonStrengths' Problem-Solving Strengths (Restorative, Input, Arranger, Analytical, Deliberative) and Traction Strengths (Focus, Activator, Command) that will help get everything moving.

Making the DBS process a "way of doing business" will help transform an organization that may be paralyzed with fear around problems and threats. Following this clear process and tapping into the appropriate strengths of each person, organizations will generate the energy to move forward to peak performance in all aspects of Octane.

Peak performance in its simplest form can be defined in the following formula:

Peak Performance = (Individual + Team Capacity) - Interferences

DBS addresses interference proactively through an action-oriented process that removes barriers to high performance. *How else can an organization ensure peak performance? What are some other elements of Octane an organization must apply?*

CONTINUOUS IMPROVEMENT

After clearly setting the foundation through AEF and the process of DBS, the organization needs to focus on Continuous Improvement (CI) to achieve true peak performance. While CI covers all areas of the POISED Model, it represents an essential factor for Octane: if you (and the organization) are not improving, you are standing still . . . which means you are falling behind everyone else who is improving. This makes CI a vital ingredient in Octane for all organizations who apply the POISED Model for success.

Applying a CI perspective assists in developing a deeper understanding of the peak performance formula. The Yerkes-Dodson Law provides an excellent assessment tool to help assess and to direct efforts for overarching CI goals: *as stress increases, performance improves; beyond a certain level of stress, performance decreases.* The following diagram illustrates this law.

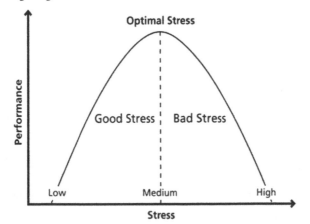

Through understanding and embodying the Yerkes-Dodson Law, and using the POISED Model, the organization's people-focused CI will accelerate and team member growth will increase more rapidly. We should recognize and ensure our people, teams, and organization advance CI efforts and reach peak performance through:

- Engagement—fostering an environment with bad stress inhibits optimal performance; strong individual and team training is vital to alleviate bad stress and to achieve a positive, collaborative environment
- Strengths-based, high-performance culture—creating an environment for better results with people doing what they do best and enjoy most
- Leadership behavior—modeling the values and behaviors critical to organizational success

We also must address the challenges that add stress and create barriers to optimal performance including:

- Significant people issues, particularly gaps in AEF
- Serious lack of alignment, especially to MV^2
- Not doing the right things and not addressing team and organizational issues
- Unclear progress measures, and unclearly communicated progress
- Unclear strategy for future success, or strategic aims not led or followed
- Uncertain source of sustained profit to reinvest in the organization
- Lack of opportunity for people to work to their potential and use their strengths

Leaders have responsibility to add Octane to the People that fuel the organization's drive for sustained high performance—and to avoid killing performance or losing people through untenable stress. Leaders who consider the Yerkes-Dodson Law and employ the principles of AEF and DBS will expedite efficiency, growth, profitability, and overall improvement. Taking actions to optimize beneficial stress for the entire organization will help increase team member engagement and job satisfaction.

Taking actions to optimize stress for the entire organization will help increase team member engagement and job satisfaction.

Organizations striving for peak performance through CI focus the organization's energy and resources to accomplish their strategic goals as they create real growth opportunities for every team member. Here are some additional considerations for carrying out people-focused CI:

- Strategic HR Management efforts with an assigned executive leader
- Professional Development Plans (PDP) for every person
- Professional Improvement Plans (PIP) for individuals as needed
- Regular and robust schedule for leadership training, team building, skills building, and other learning
- Prioritized improvement projects for every team across all functions
- Succession planning

Placing emphasis on implementing strong HR practices can elevate everyone in the organization. The traditional organization thinks of the HR function as a necessary group to hire, fire, and deal with difficult people situations. In the POISED Model, great HR becomes a high-performance enabler and differentiator for optimizing People and Octane, freeing employees throughout the organization to function at higher and higher levels. The Strategic HR Plan process deserves a prioritized place in the team's rhythm of the business and is covered in additional detail later in this book (Chapters 4 and 6).

Embedded in the practice of CI is a commitment to be a learning organization, as defined by Peter Senge in his monumental leadership book, *The Fifth Discipline*[6]. Senge described such organizations as places "where people continually expand their capacity to create the results they truly desire, where new and expansive patterns of thinking are nurtured, where collective aspiration is set free, and where people are continually learning how to learn together."

The learning-organization concept embodies the fundamental purpose outcome of learning: to create a positive change in behavior. A learning organization effectively manages knowledge (creating, identifying, storing, and transferring knowledge) and consistently modifies its behavior to reflect new knowledge and insights (improving processes, solving tactical problems, and achieving strategic goals).

Practicing CI with a direct focus on being a learning organization means everyone sees continuous and positive changes in what is being done, resulting in elevated Octane for the organization, its people, and its results.

Octane is the People fuel additive that boosts increased performance and enables true transformational leaders to make it happen. Transformational leaders create authentic, lasting, and positive change while developing the next generation of leaders who will do the same.

Leadership adding the highest level of Octane to the team trumps the strengths of one or a few strong leaders. A strong, well-fueled team will accomplish and sustain the greatest results—not a singular leader, person, or entity who may find fleeting success. Leaders who love their people with a full expression of servant leadership—and pour themselves into their team members' development and the development of the business—will optimize Octane for individual and collective success.

Are you ready? Are there "miracles" waiting for you? Do you have the Octane to lead you forward? Maybe you and your organization are not facing the juggernaut Soviet Union Olympic hockey team who had not lost in Olympic play for more than 20 years, but whomever or whatever you face, with the right Octane you have the opportunity to push forward.

If you build the POISED Model into your organization, and implement the People and Octane practices we highlight, the culture of continuous improvement and learning you create will generate the Octane your team needs to accomplish your miracle.

Now, with your strong foundation of People and Octane in place, move forward to Chapter 3 and Identify the critical priorities, needs, and objectives you must tackle on your high-performance journey.

POISED® Key Points Summary	
People	Develop each person to their fullest capability and enable optimal utilization of their Strengths
Octane	. . . of the organization – Mission, Vision, Values (MV^2) – and results driven, shaped through continuous improvement in all facets of the organization
Identify	
Strategy	
Engine of Profitability	
Do	
POISED® Integrated Model	

3

IDENTIFY

"If you don't know where you are going,
you might find yourself someplace else."
–Yogi Berra, Hall of Fame Baseball Player–

Identifying priorities for action while choosing what NOT to do is key for effective strategy. And, if you want your team members to contribute to meaningful work toward a vision larger than themselves, prioritization is essential. When we use the word "priority", we mean intentional, key actions critical to success.

In his book *First Things First*, Stephen Covey labeled priorities "big rocks" and often used an on-stage demonstration of filling a jar with sand and small pebbles, showing that the big rocks no longer fit in the jar when small nuisances or busy work (sand and pebbles) filled the space[7]. Covey reminds us to put the big rocks in FIRST.

Have you Identified your team's and organization's big rock priorities—and what sand and pebbles you should bypass? The next step in the POISED Model is Identifying priorities, an intentional selection of key actions that focus the organization's People and Octane.

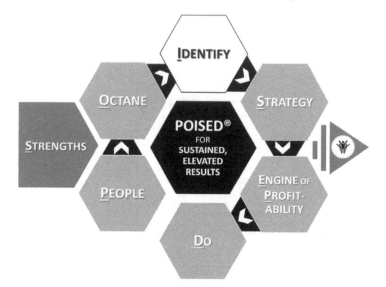

LEADERSHIP STORY

In a true story from ship diaries entitled *The Light and the Glory*, we learn about the long, arduous, dangerous, and inspiring historical landing of the Pilgrims. We extract a few segments from the chronicles of this exciting adventure to provide an emphasis on the importance of the Identify element of the POISED Model. We turn to a riveting section:

> *Suddenly, a tremendous boom resounded through the ship. The main crossbeam supporting the main mast had cracked and was sagging alarmingly. . . Master Jones himself came to see. From the look on his face, it was obvious to the Pilgrims that the situation was as ominous as they had feared.*

Then Brewster remembered the great iron screw of his printing press. It was on-board somewhere. A desperate search was begun. Finally, it was located, dug out, hauled into place under the sagging beam, and cranked up. It met the beam and, to the accompaniment of a hideous creaking and groaning of the wood, began to raise it—all the way back to its original position[8].

This quotation summarizes one of the incredible battles, including unending vicious storms at sea, overcome by the Pilgrims as they sailed in 1620 to the new world, their mission to escape religious tyranny during that time in Europe.

But this was not the only challenge on sea.

At last, on November 9 the words they had waited so long to hear rang out from the lookout: "Land ho!" They rushed up on the main deck, where they caught their first glimpse of a long, sandy stretch of coastline, covered with dune grass and scrub pine. One of the pilots identified it as a place the fishermen called Cape Cod. Despite the seemingly endless storm, they had actually been blown less than a hundred miles off their course—north, as it turned out. It should have taken them only a day to round the elbow of the Cape and perhaps three more days to reach the mouth of the Hudson.

They turned south.

But at the Cape's elbow, Monomoy Point, there are fierce shoals and riptides. And with the heavy headwinds they now faced, the going became progressively more treacherous. Finally, after battling the wall of wind for two days, Master Jones said that before attempting to proceed further south, he would have to head out to sea and wait another day.

At length, and after much prayer and further discussion, they instructed Master Jones to turn about and make for the northern tip of the Cape (Provincetown). This he did, and on November 11, they dropped anchor in the natural harbor just inside the Cape.

At this point, a new question arose: if they were to settle here, they would no longer be under the jurisdiction of the Virginia Company . . . [T]his thought stirred rebellion in the hearts of some of the strangers, and the Pilgrim leaders realized they had to act quickly and decisively to forestall the very real possibility of mutiny.

Their solution was pragmatic and expedient. It took into consideration. . . human nature. . . [t]hey drafted a Compact . . . which embodied the principles of equality and government by the consent of the governed.

The Mayflower Compact would become the cornerstone of American government[9].

Let us take this bit of history and summarize a few of the enormous challenges faced by the Pilgrims as we have read from these excerpts:

- An incredibly long storm accompanied them, severely delaying their trip across the Atlantic Ocean
- The storm was so severe that they were hit with a crack in the main crossbeam supporting the main mast—effectively demobilizing their ship and preventing completion of their mission—likely at the cost of their lives if not fixed

- They were forced to head back to sea, given the peril of the shoals and riptides and the heavy headwinds, when they longed to land on shore
- They were faced with mutiny when their landing was about 100 miles from their legally supported destination

We want to use this true story to emphasize what was truly important to the Pilgrims. They had to focus on the most important things needed to survive, to accomplish their mission, and ultimately thrive. In these vivid historically documented situations, it is evident the Pilgrims understood the need to *Identify the critical factors for their mission and act intentionally.*

In your organization, our POISED Model expects you will always do the same.

PRIORITY FOCUS

We introduce the Identify component of the POISED Model with an emphasis on developing a summary priority area list. It is always critical, even before focusing on monitoring, allocating resources, teaming to accomplish, and ultimately doing what is needed, to Identify the most important, prioritized areas for action.

The elements POISED emphasizes to Identify are:

- Key strategic initiatives and implementation actions
- Most important areas to measure, most cost-effectively, and for highest benefit
- Key areas should always include a client, employee, and continuous improvement urgency, with quality and safety at the forefront
- Processes should be prioritized for focus and improvement

- Blind spots and assumptions that limit effective decision-making
- Threats from external (competitive, regulatory, economic, societal, etc.) or internal (human resource, budgetary, cultural, etc.) sources that may limit or prevent success
- Solutions focus on emerging critical needs to address, through DBS and leaders' prioritization
- All POISED elements are clearly incorporated in the areas we Identify

Throughout *The Light and the Glory*, and in the sections quoted, we see the Pilgrims through their leaders addressing their mission in a strategic way: to establish a new home free from the religious persecution they fled. We also see them identifying short- and long-term priorities related to achievement of their vision, as documented in ships' diaries and ultimately in the drafting of a Compact to avoid instituting another powerful autocratic governance system.

From the Pilgrims' urgent actions to fix their perilous broken mast problem, to their extensive prayerful discussions and subsequent actions around governance at a new unauthorized landing, the Pilgrims identified and pursued critically important priorities. They were clear about:

1. A new governing structure (Strategic priorities)
2. Solutions-focus addressing (Business) challenges
3. Fixing equipment needed for sailing (Processes) most in need of improvement

Lessons from the Pilgrims' decisions reflect our emphasis on Identify. They engaged their focus on key strategic initiatives (like the Compact), applied resources to address emerging critical issues (storms, mast cracking, preventing landing, mutiny), and later used metrics on food allocation to measure activities critical to survival. They also relied on functional leadership, such as the technical leadership of ship leader Master Jones, organizational leadership of the Pilgrims, and the HR/spiritual leadership of a particular leader. Their journey presents useful, poignant examples of the need to Identify to be successful—even to survive—and then to be poised to thrive.

CRITICAL CHOICES

POISED emphasizes that you ensure the organization devotes energy to and spends time on key activities based on the correct priorities identified in your strategy, current and future strategic priorities, and through properly identified/selected metrics to focus resources where they will make the biggest difference. Prioritize all items for optimal productivity and results, now and in the future.

 Choosing the responsible team, metric owner, and senior champion is critical for identifying, simplifying, and tracking metrics effectively and efficiently.

With this focus as a foundation, you and your organization then can:

- Select important measures representing a balance of client, quality, learning, people-focus, and results processes and outcomes
- Align selected performance measures to key mission, vision, and strategic priorities

- Recognize the importance of continuously improving and simplifying the tracking, reporting, and analysis of performance measures
- Gain early wins by focusing on "low-hanging fruit"
- Implement steps to deploy measures efficiently and effectively across units (horizontally) and through organizational levels (vertically), which improves the focus of senior leaders and all employees
- Invest smartly in efficient technology to facilitate knowledge management, especially in the open sharing of clear, simplified, and impactful metrics

Choosing the responsible team, metric owner, and senior champion is critical for identifying, simplifying, and tracking metrics effectively and efficiently. The senior champion must possess the right background and strengths to inspire organizational action, to remove barriers and provide resources, and to communicate performance gaps and success. Specifying who owns the metric (collects, displays, and analyzes the data) is critical to convert data and information to knowledge. And, a well-rounded/critical-strengths-included team is vital to focus operational activity on processes that influence performance reflected by the metric.

Each sales, delivery, and functional leader should drive and assure identification, tracking, simplification, and communication of action-oriented measures and priorities with a continued focus on operational excellence throughout the business. Ensuring product/service quality and employee/community safety receive attention and ownership by all are integral to meaningful metrics and a high-performance culture. The DBS tool (Appendix), used when an important business issue emerges, will often identify the priority business improvement areas.

Have you taken the time to Identify the proper priorities in your strategic plan? Are these reflected in your weekly meetings and your individual one-on-one meetings with your team? If you truly live your mission, and you and your team strive to achieve your vision, you will want to be sure you can answer, "YES!"

Operational and strategic priority success requires engagement at all levels, starting with clarity and ownership to Identify, prioritize, and drive focus on key processes and business improvement areas. Choose your direction deliberately, then put resources and people to work to achieve your strategy. Now, let us dive into the design of Strategy in Chapter 4.

POISED® Key Points Summary	
People	Develop each person to their fullest capability and enable optimal utilization of their Strengths
Octane	. . . of the organization – Mission, Vision, Values (MV²) – and results driven, shaped through continuous improvement in all facets of the organization
Identify	**. . . all priorities, challenges, opportunities, and metrics – to act with wise use of resources**
Strategy	
Engine of Profitability	
Do	
POISED® Integrated Model	

4

STRATEGY

*"Strategy is about making choices, trade-offs;
it's about deliberately choosing to be different."*
−Michael Porter, Author, Harvard Business School−

Do you have a strategy? Is it a winning strategy for your team? Is it working for the success of your organization? Strategy is the thread that runs through a forward-looking organization. It converts vision (where we want to go in the future) into actions (what we must change or transform to get there) that enable mission (what we do and why we do it).

In typical organizations, strategic plans end up gathering dust on a shelf. Even strategy-focused organizations that create an overarching plan often fall short in their execution. The key to develop and implement an effective strategic plan is to set *long-range objectives* in a time horizon appropriate to the organization, then define, pursue, and monitor *short-range actions* that change or improve the business model and the organization's services/products, programs, process, and operations.

Now let us walk through Strategy, starting first with a story, then outlining the approach you can follow for a successful strategy.

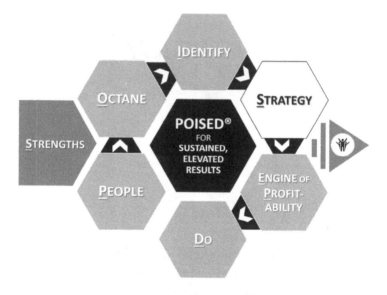

LEADERSHIP STORY

Nehemiah, a prophet of Israel, was in Babylonian captivity[10]. While in captivity his heart and spirit were moved to help restore Israel, his home, to what it was once before: GREAT, A NATIONAL POWER. In approaching this overarching goal strategically, he began with a major strategic step. He identified, prioritized, and planned to rebuild the wall around Jerusalem which had been destroyed as Israel was defeated and taken into captivity (first Identify key issues, Chapter 3).

He approached the wall rebuilding through the following strategic steps:

- Have a strategic plan that considers resources (he asked the king for letters to the governor who could provide timber for the gates)
- Identify and determine key priorities based on careful evaluation of the situation (environmental scan)
- Have a solid unifying foundation to engage his people and others built on a shared mission, vision, and values
- Utilize the unique strengths of the people around him while capitalizing on partner-up opportunities with strategic leaders and other important groups and entities
- Understand the "markets" within which he worked—satisfying the captors of Babylon, the people whose home he wished to restore (Israelites), and the competing markets against him (other countries that hated Israel)
- Collaborated with internal team members and groups as well as the needed external partners-suppliers
- Examined challenges and opportunities systematically and then developed a comprehensive, specific strategic plan to accomplish the complete rebuild in 52 days; he began with the end in mind and worked backwards through the granular details to ensure complete success
- Then in the end, after completing the plan, he and his people celebrated their win and looked to the next iteration of planning for complete and full restoration of his people, his home, and his country

Why were his strategies so successful? What does it take to have an effective strategy? What can we do to generate the right strategy to accomplish the great goals we desire for ourselves and our organizations?

As we overview the Strategy element of POISED, we will help answer the age-old question of what makes a great strategy set for victory.

STRATEGY BUILDING BLOCKS

Where should your organization's strategy start? It all starts with an internal look at the Mission, Vision, and Values (MV²). Every organization must build its Strategy on a clear foundation of MV². After all, a strategy that does not align closely with MV² just takes an organization's people, resources, and actions off course.

Therefore, start Strategy development by reviewing and rewriting or modifying, as needed, the MV². These elements must be compelling and inspiring. Their wording must be clear and direct, with their themes understood and followed by everyone on the team. They should be reflected strongly in the delivery of services/products your organization provides to the clients you serve. They also need to be built on your organizational strengths and operational excellence which will help you to excel.

Do not get caught up in the semantic definitions of MV². The many different definitions and applications of these terms confuse people and distract them from the importance of the concepts. Therefore, just use the following simple concepts to frame and to articulate the important foundational pieces for your Strategy:

- Mission—speaks to what and why you do what you do
- Vision—speaks to where you are taking your Mission in the future
- Values—speak to your foundational ideals that everything your organization does must reflect

Once you have set your clear, unifying, and driving force embodied in the MV² foundation, the next steps in Strategy can occur. Next, assess the external market and the needs that exist, are evolving, or may be anticipated or even created. Examine what customers need (now and in the future). An effective strategy, first and foremost, focuses on the identified and anticipated needs of customers today and in the future.

How do we best serve our customers? A customer-focused organization clearly determines and defines its Unique Selling Points (USPs)—those service/product attributes, delivery competencies, and service/product features that differentiate you from others in the marketplace. USPs always stem from the organization's strengths, core competencies, and hard-to-emulate capabilities.

Customers (those who you serve) reside within, and sometimes across, different markets. Markets could be based on unique customer characteristics, specific service/product expectations, geographies, or other defining factors. To underpin a strong customer-focused strategy, clearly examine and determine your chosen key market(s) that emphasize and leverage your "niche" or core competencies (what are you really good at doing). Continue to use MV^2 as a filter to work through these decision points, which then provide a framework for you to define specific objectives and establish measurable, positive goals for individuals and the entire organization.

KEY STRATEGY INPUTS

The strategy-focused organization also will want to collect and to analyze data and information about other external market pieces directly addressing critical financial constraints and opportunities (Engine of Profitability, Chapter 5). To generate an effective and targeted strategy, the organization needs to focus on and examine:

- The competition and their services/products and chosen markets
- New entrants into the market and their potential financial and competitive impact on your organization

- Supply trends for workers, materials, and products
- Local, regional, and global trends and potential impacts
- Regulatory and policy requirements and trends
- Other strategic partners, collaborators, and vendors
- Identified and anticipated customer needs and trends

This examination of selected strategic inputs, commonly termed an "environmental scan", provides a fact-based understanding of the factors your strategic planning must consider. To place a finer point on these inputs, synthesize them into two sets based on how they may influence your organization:

- Strategic advantages—*benefits* that exert a decisive influence on your organization's likelihood of future success; these advantages are frequently sources of current and future competitive success relative to other providers of similar services/products
- Strategic challenges—*pressures* that exert a decisive influence on your organization's likelihood of future success; these challenges are frequently driven by your organization's anticipated competitive position in the future relative to other providers of similar products and also can include internal challenges

Strategic advantages and challenges represent knowledge and support a strong fact-based foundation. With this foundation, you may clearly define potential specific goals and desired steps to carry out in your Strategy. Your Strategy will focus on leveraging your strengths, capitalizing on strategic advantages, minimizing or eliminating strategic challenges, and articulating priorities that enable the organization to achieve the Vision.

Now that you have established your internal foundation and external market considerations, you begin to conduct a simple but important examination of Challenges and Opportunities for your organization (Identify). Many organizations will be tempted to conduct a SWOT Analysis (Strengths, Weaknesses, Opportunities, and Threats). In our practice, we choose a more direct method than this often time-consuming and cumbersome approach.

Too often, groups spend weeks to months in a SWOT analysis. Instead, simply focus on two factors:

1. *Challenges*—potential issues impeding your forward movement
2. *Opportunities*—potential possibilities you must act upon to seize momentum, grow your organization, and realize success

This simplification allows the organization to take action more rapidly. We recommend you gather the top three to five Challenges and Opportunities from your key, most knowledgeable leaders involved in setting your Strategy, rank them in importance from 4 (vitally important) to 1 (real but not a high priority), and then order them from highest to lowest priority. These priorities readily convert into measurable goals for your Strategy—after additional filtering based on additional organizational factors.

In addition to factoring the Challenges and Opportunities directly into the organization's strategy, we highly emphasize the importance of focusing on the organization's strengths. Rather than building your strategy based solely on external factors, consider your internal strengths (e.g., Strengths and Opportunities) as a filter. Emphasize your organization's strengths to focus your energies for maximum success and true engagement of your people. An organization's strengths drive a tailored winning strategy to ensure success. And, when an organization faces gaps it must address to achieve its Strategy, strengths provide a firm and steady foundation from which to fill those gaps.

An organization's strengths drive a tailored winning strategy to ensure success. And, when an organization faces gaps it must address to achieve its Strategy, strengths provide a firm and steady foundation from which to fill those gaps.

Internal finances represent a final and crucial area to analyze before you set specific strategic goals. Economic trends and financial conditions likely will arise during your Challenges and Opportunities assessment, but a specific deep-dive into your finances helps bring your overall strategy picture into focus including an historical financial perspective, a current plan, and a 3- to 5-year future financial projection.

Every organization should conduct a detailed deep-dive into its financials to gain a clear understanding of where you have been, where you stand currently, and where you plan to go. The clearer your financial metrics align to strategic priorities (Chapter 5, Engine of Profitability)—with meaningful and repeatable reporting and analysis—the better your chances for achieving your winning Strategy. In addition, financial analysis delivers a shared understanding of what resources you have available to build reality-based action plans for your strategy. Armed with the realities of your finances and clear, communicated metrics, now you may step forward to set specific strategic goals.

CONVERTING STRATEGY INTO ACTION

A Strategy without specific goals is a recipe for frustration and failure. Fortunately, this common problem boils down to a straight-forward solution: break down long-range strategies into actionable goals, each assigned to a senior champion, and each with an identified short-term timeline progress, outcome metrics, and dedicated financial and human resources. This is the *organization's work* required for strategic success.

To set effective strategic goals, every organization should assess its past approach to strategy and articulate its new strategic framework: customer focus with a clearly defined niche, MV^2 (as updated), with a simple and clear statement of Strategy (how we best utilize our precious resources—people, time, money, leadership attention—to achieve our vision). Applying this framework will keep you aligned with all other aspects of POISED.

The right Strategy accounts for and considers every aspect of the POISED Model. You may not go into the depth and detail as when you focus on each POISED component singly; however, your final goal setting likely will have one or more strategic goals derived from each POISED component.

In articulating your strategic approach to enable implementation, you will begin to focus on some of the following key factors:

- Your organizational model and how you lead delivery and serve clients
- Your leadership structure and how those in key roles best support execution of the Strategy
- Your organization's portfolio of service and product offerings and choices
- Your emphasis on execution, operational excellence, sales, and marketing
- Your commitment to customer focus including customer feedback (satisfaction and complaints), services/products, technologies, and costs

Remember, in setting and implementing Strategy, use your Fuel Meeting (detailed in Chapter 6 and the Appendix) to keep leadership regularly focused on strategic priorities in your plan. Utilize the other tools and resources such as AEF, DBS, Strengths, and other POISED elements. Strategy brings it all together.

As you set goals (see Appendix, Strategic Plan Template), we recommend the following format and sequencing:

1. Start with establishing where you want to be in the future (Vision)
2. Use the highest-rated Challenges and Opportunities to shape the specific goals you choose (capitalize on Strategic Advantages and minimize or eliminate Strategic Challenges in framing the specific goals)
3. Convert long-range priorities into shorter-term actions with a cascading approach
   a. Define 6-year goals as a recommended long-range starting point
   b. Build 3-year goals designed to track achievement of each 6-year goal
   c. Create a 1-year goal designed to track completion of each desired 3-year goal
   d. Set 90-day goals to drive toward accomplishment of each 1-year goal
4. Formalize the leadership and operational plan
   a. Name an Executive Team member as senior champion for each 6- and 3-year goal
   b. Assign a specific owner to each 1-year and 90-day goal (Do in the POISED Model) responsible to make sure the goal is completed; they do not have to personally

accomplish the entire goal, but they will report on its progress and ensure completion of this goal

c.   Load financial, human, and other key resources into each 90-day and 1-year action plan

Congratulations! Now your team has designed its Strategy and you are ready to hit the ground running. Remember, the Strategy you have established represents a living plan, a living document. Each strategic priority and goal (from long-range Vision down to the 90-day action plans) must be monitored and reported organizationally and may be changed or modified as needed to keep you tracking toward your strategic destination.

 Strategy is not meant to be a stagnant constraining theory developed for everyone to look at and marvel. Strategy guides, directs, and assists your organization in moving with agility and in achieving victory proactively through a winning Strategy.

At minimum, you must review performance every 90 days and you may change, revise, and adjust as needed. Strategy is not meant to be a stagnant constraining theory developed for everyone to look at and marvel. Strategy guides, directs, and assists your organization in moving with agility and in achieving victory proactively through a winning Strategy.

As you conclude each 1-year goal, make sure you celebrate achievement, assess what went right and what could be better, review the Strategy in its entirety, and adjust (or reinvent) it as determined beneficial to accommodate actual and anticipated changes in the external and internal landscape. A strategy-focused organization builds this habit and repeats this pattern each 90 days, every year, year after year, as it carries out its Strategy and achieves success.

WINNING STRATEGY

Strategy encompasses all facets of the POISED Model. Your organization sets it in place to ensure a win for all stakeholders, with a focus built on the foundation of MV^2 and a POISED approach emphasizing:

- Team-based Strategic Plan (see Appendix, Strategic Plan Template) development and team buy-in, recognizing leadership has choices and decisions to make
- A clear Strategic Plan with four to six ("vital few" rather than "trivial many") well-defined strategic priorities that drive progress toward the Vision and position the organization for results and sustained, elevated performance
- Individual and team ownership and a process to drive accountability for the action plan
- Emphasis on regular, consistent, and appropriate communication of the Strategic Plan to all constituencies

The POISED elements used through this Strategy overview will help ensure you are headed on the path to ultimate victory—with an ability to adjust as needed to ultimately realize true and meaningful success.

Just as Nehemiah engineered a winning strategy to lead to ultimate victory, you can and you will do the same. You will utilize a strong foundation, built on a unifying mission and vision to accomplish work through the strengths of all team members, while taking into account internal and external factors that enable you to generate actionable goals. Your Strategic Plan is ready for prime time.

What is next? We will take a deeper look into the "E" of POISED—the Engine of Profitability—in Chapter 5.

POISED® Key Points Summary	
People	Develop each person to their fullest capability and enable optimal utilization of their Strengths
Octane	. . . of the organization – Mission, Vision, Values (MV^2) – and results driven, shaped through continuous improvement in all facets of the organization
Identify	. . . all priorities, challenges, opportunities, and metrics – to act with wise use of resources
Strategy	. . . to leverage Strengths to win for all facets of the organization, clearly communicated to all constituencies and acted upon
Engine of Profitability	
Do	
POISED® Integrated Model	

5

THE ENGINE OF
PROFITABILITY

*"If you focus on the goal and not the process,
you inevitably compromise. For me, profit is
what happens when you do everything else right."*
–Yvon Chouinard, Patagonia Founder–

All organizations of any type and every size—for-profit, charity/not-for-profit, religious, educational, or governmental, from conglomerate to sole proprietorships—operate on the same fundamental principle of economic sustainability. They either provide value to customers, stakeholders, and constituents to build financial resources, or they do not. They either sustain the organization as a going concern or they do not survive.

Survival is optional and leaders must choose to fuel the Engine of Profitability (EoP) with the right blend of strategic, operational, and human additives—for the benefit of those they serve and the good of the communities in which they work. Once leaders choose to fuel and then continuously tune the EoP, they face one other significant question: how to pursue and maintain profitability through a holistic focus on process, people, and principles.

The road to profitability is neither good nor bad, but the approaches to get there and what an organization does at the destination say everything about its virtue and values. So, make money with your EoP; do it the right way and then do right with the money you make.

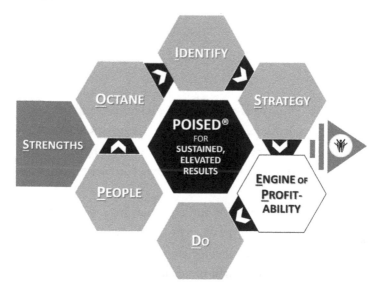

LEADERSHIP STORY

Mark's father (LeRoy Christian Wrightsman, or Chris) understood the meaning of the POISED EoP element as he built three startup printing companies starting in the 1960s and extending into the 1970s and 1980s. Dad understood that minimizing his capital outlay by buying used but functional printing presses, cutters, folders, and other printing equipment of the era, then leveraging manual labor (like mine) to clean them and to provide lots of tender, loving care, represented a low startup cost. He also drove for pricing in customer proposals to ensure good margins, considering all costs and taking into account the market and competition for each type of printing produced.

For Dad, this lowest-investment approach made good business sense, but it was also necessary because he had very minimal savings at the time. He understood even more the critical elements of cash flow driven by cost-efficient operations and timely collections to stay afloat and to feed a family of seven—following an earlier personal bankruptcy experience before starting his first company. He focused smartly on getting a fair price from customers for printed material such as brochures, forms, advertising, and letterheads; being efficient at production; and sourcing paper, ink, and other materials at reasonable costs. Providing quality printing on-time also meant he could collect on a timely basis and keep funding the business for growth.

While it did not all dawn on me then as a kid, Dad knew the key elements of EoP. And I simply did what was expected to contribute: I filled offset-press oil reservoirs and then, on my hands and knees, sopped up machine particle-filled oil from under these old presses, intricate and well-running machines but with worn bearings and leaky oil traps near the floor, and collated books and other forms and printed material. More insight and learnings came over time from Dad's repetitive experiences as he started one business in Minneapolis, one in Fort Lauderdale, and another later in Punta Gorda in southwest Florida. In each subsequent startup, he leveraged deeper experience and greater self-funding capability. He created success at each one through his commitment, beginning with his first company when he often stayed overnight, napping on his worn canvas Army cot before getting back to work.

I benefitted in my early teens not only from Dad letting me eventually run machines and perform many tasks required in a printing company, but even more so from absorbing my father's energetically communicated daily business lessons about making, saving, and investing money to build his business. Expecting and enabling employees to do their part, driving hard to fulfill customer needs, applying conservative financial approaches and funding—Dad led these efforts to produce consistent long-term results as the businesses' leader and then enthusiastically rehashed these experiences and stories with family and friends. These were all extraordinary teaching points for us.

As we provide examples from our experience in this chapter to help communicate the need for extraordinary urgency around the EoP—a holistic and value-creating financial imperative—we ask you to think about and to gain insight from your own experiences. Many of us learn best while doing and reflecting on these experiences while you read is the next best thing. We have intentionally included many different business examples, making this chapter a bit longer and, hopefully, also clearer as you relate to your own unique experiences.

FUELING THE ENGINE

When in your career was there such a singular focus on current, near-term results in a business that the longer-term, beneficial EoP was neglected?

When in your experience was the focus on the dream, the mission, and the excitement so consuming that the financial engine was ignored?

Have you worked in or observed a business ultimately head towards failure, and did you see the mission focus die slowly as funds dwindled?

We place a significant emphasis on the value-creating EoP aspect of the POISED Model to prevent these unwanted and ineffectual outcomes. We intentionally start this chapter by providing several organizational examples that highlight business-specific EoP implementation to build a broad and strong foundation.

EoP Spotlight: Sophisticated Technical Service Business

I fast forward from my childhood experience in my father's printing business to General Electric's (GE's) Nuclear business after college. This GE business was formed in 1955 as the Atomic Power Equipment Department. When I joined in 1980, the year Jack Welch arrived in the CEO office, a new message was clear and the focus shifted dramatically. Welch's message in his first business review (with people well above my entry-level engineering program management position) was emphatic: *NO MORE PLANNING FOR A NEW UNIT SALE THAT WILL 'PERHAPS' MAKE MONEY! We do NOT run a development organization. We do NOT want more unit plant orders. Get the young Service business supporting the fleet going, drive the Fuel business, and run them as a PROFITABLE GE business.*

The message that we should not expect more new unit plant orders reverberated across the entire organization and became the reality for a long time. We needed to run the business segments that we had profitably. A momentous event left another indelible business-lesson imprint in my young career when I was one of the fortunate GE Nuclear employees who received a small wood and black engraved plaque reading "In the black in 1981!" after a successful year doing as Jack mandated. Jack set the bar, but GE Nuclear's own leadership team developed and implemented the plans and celebrated the successes including—finally, after more than 25 years—making a profit!

The GE Nuclear business cultivated a strong focus on cost structure for growing a profitable product and service business that included engineering services, control room electronics upgrades, and other services to support plant operation and outages. Each of these nuclear plant support areas eventually were considered distinctive business segments with specific segment drivers and with profit margins corresponding to the value of their product or service. All were sold through account leaders facing operating utility clients directly.

The transformation of this "aftermarket" business, as well as the high-technology nuclear fuel design and manufacturing business, became core to a profitable GE Nuclear business with clear, definable profit generators. For instance, the scope of engineering solutions provided to support Power Uprates and Plant Life Extensions (PLEX) was something only GE Nuclear could perform for utility clients with GE-supplied plants. Eventually, these Uprates and PLEX offerings became key to one of the highest-margin businesses for GE Nuclear, as clients could achieve new increments of valuable electric power production capacity for a very low investment cost compared to building a new plant.

GE won . . . and clients won even bigger. Focus on this particular EoP offering was one key element in accelerating and strengthening the GE Nuclear business. When I earned the opportunity in 1996 to lead GE Nuclear's aftermarket business, the business had grown from around $40 million annually just as I left a product management role to become an early account manager in the mid-1980s to around $400 million in annual revenue. However, it had suffered several years of decline in revenue and profit, and it had some reputation issues with the Nuclear Regulatory Commission (NRC).

I already knew many great team members in the business and had the chance for intense briefings walking in the door. In 1996, with some very rapid reorganizations around clients and delivery, and a focus on quality and communications with the NRC, the team had an amazing year. We benefitted from a reduced cost structure going into the year. The team did a remarkable job by intentionally unleashing account managers and business leaders to focus on people and client needs.

We instilled a disciplined rhythm of accountability, and in business reviews and through consistent follow-up, assured a hyper-focus on particular areas of the EoP for each business segment. We also were driven as a team of senior leaders to provide the high-octane fuel that energized people to work hard on the year's turnaround of revenue, profit, and regulator confidence. Other chapters highlight additional dimensions of fueling the business with high octane within additional POISED elements—this is what we did to maximize our GE Nuclear aftermarket team's potential.

EoP Spotlight: Technology-Driven Industrial Capital Goods Business

I also had the opportunity to learn and to experience new areas as I moved first to the Asia region and next to the Europe/Middle East Region in GE's Power Systems business. It presented its own unique EoP attributes; the Power business required massive investment in technology features, including specialty materials and designs and, for decades, had worked to be the leader in producing high-efficiency turbine generators.

Over time, the parts, service, and upgrades aftermarket business became a larger and larger driver of success—for GE and for its clients. Utility clients benefitted from optimized maintenance, helping them achieve the highest capacity factor so critical to their economics along with cost savings from GE's highly efficient turbine generators.

Central to GE's global-growth strategy, many of us moved to Singapore, Hong Kong, Japan, or Europe as part of GE Power's Nuovo Pignone acquisition and integration. Growing globally through strategic partnering and strong sales teams to solidify worldwide market share were critical to achieve a massive revenue scale through new unit sales and required to fund the continuous R&D investment to establish and to maintain a market leadership position.

Profitability resulted from the thoughtful combination of these elements to generate the necessary revenue. Product Management and Engineering competencies ensured successful innovative new product introductions, supported by global sales to help drive winning positions, aligned to fine-tune GE Power's EoP. Over time, the higher-margin global aftermarket segment became even more important, providing profit to fuel the next development cycles and fleet growth.

EoP Spotlight: Automotive Business

After nearly 17 years of GE experiences, I transitioned into a global business leadership role at SPX, an automotive-centric business at the time, enriching my experience with a deep-dive education in this industry. The automotive industry led in development of leaner, quality-driven successful companies; those that did not pursue this direction often were left in the dust.

For highly competitive industries such as automotive production and sales, getting ahead in the organization's EoP focus *and staying ahead* are critical. Toyota's famous Toyota Production System (TPS) is the subject of a number of good business books that are great resources for examining an automotive industry leader's EoP (with great lessons for any industry). Toyota created a unique and profitable lean production model for its EoP by relentlessly focusing on client value and product development, integrating suppliers into the earliest stages of new designs, and intertwining every aspect of the business starting and ending with clients.

Once the TPS EoP became a humming flywheel, it established a resoundingly high-quality product reputation with rapid production cycle times that drove increasing market share and sustained revenue and profit growth. The winning cost position that resulted from their TPS processes, with pricing capacity given their vehicle's premier reputation in the marketplace, led to a strong EoP and perpetual competitive leadership. Toyota's results and processes are worth learning from and modeling; from their start not too many decades ago, their amazing performance compares very favorably and places them ahead of longer-tenured U.S. auto producers.

EoP Spotlight: Internet Security Software Startup

This example could be subtitled "how to fund your company existence while building your product from concept to production." It serves as a strong example of balancing investment in innovation with consistent financial growth.

On January 1, 1997, four men who abandoned their day jobs—Jay Johnson, Jay Chaudhry, Richard Rushing, and Phil Agcaoili—started a company called SecureIT in Atlanta, Georgia, based on an idea of building internet security services and products for the emerging internet commerce world.

Like most blazing entrepreneurs, they knew what they wanted to build but did not know how to solve their biggest challenge of funding their company's existence while it invented its product/service. No bank would consider giving them a loan, nor would outside investors fund the idea, considering it a high-risk paper business plan at this phase. So, the founders decided to self-fund the business, betting that they could generate organic revenue to fund the business plan.

Their short-term business plan to generate revenue and profit involved becoming Internet Security Consultants to the Fortune

1000, focused on a service of identifying security threats and closing them. As they surfaced customer opportunities, they quickly realized most businesses did not believe they had an Internet Security problem and were forced to educate their audience about security before they could have the opportunity to sell security solutions to them. They were very early to the security market—with a service even customers did not know they needed.

Now, they had to generate customer prospects while simultaneously educating them on why they needed security. They literally were building the airplane as they flew it. So, they launched a seminar series entitled "What Hackers Know That You Don't". The seminar demonstrated live how hackers find their internet targets; they showed how hackers performed reconnaissance to discover the attributes of the target's devices, operating environment, interfaces, applications, and defenses; identified the vulnerabilities of the targets to exploit; and displayed the tools hackers used to break in. The seminar series was a smash hit, and quickly grew to audiences of more than 1,000 people. Customers wanted to be educated!

In one of the seminars, AT&T attendees pulled the presenters aside and asked them to create a security education course that would address AT&T internal company technology and educate their IT member team on how to identify and to close their own vulnerabilities. The team agreed, charged them $250,000, created a one-week course for AT&T IT employees, and then started to train them on security.

They then repurposed the AT&T course and expanded it for the general commercial public to cover many technologies. They charged students $1,000 a day for a one-week course generating $5,000 in revenue per student per week. Each security trainer-consultant instructed about 12 students per class and generated $60,000 a week on average in consulting revenue. Do the math: one consultant generated $240,000 monthly in services revenue!

Next, the team hired more security practitioners to educate the world while moving forward with their business plan. The security course identified many security problems that would require many different vendor products (firewalls, intrusion detection monitors, authentication, encryption, PKI, web app filters, etc.) to resolve the security threats. They had their EoP to transport them to the next phase of their own software product development (called Secure-VIEW) and quickly became the go-to provider of security solutions to the Fortune 100. Just 18 months after its launch, SecureIT was sold to Verisign (VRSN) in July 1998 for $69 million.

EoP Spotlight: Private Equity Owned Robotics Business

Now we return to Mark's experience. From my time late in high school working at Kentucky Fried Chicken (KFC) restaurants to save for college, where managing labor cost, reducing waste, and maintaining consumer satisfaction were EoP keys, to my time engaged in GE assignments and almost 20 years leading PaR Systems, a complex Robotics business, it became clear that sustainability and long-term success in every organization came down to keeping a trained eye on EoP. Identifying EoP factors, keeping a focus on the critical business aspects, and optimizing the operation holistically is both essential and critical to sustain the business.

By 1999, when I was chosen to lead PaR Systems, the company had become a modestly profitable private-equity-held business, recovering from very challenging financial years earlier in the decade. We knew that designing, building, installing, and servicing robotics and automated material handling equipment was subject to swings in the capital-goods buying cycles. Our team set forth a strategy of diversifying markets to avoid single industry cycles. We moved full speed ahead on driving technology and finding robotic solutions to solve application needs demanded by clients in each chosen segment. We invested to ensure a growing after-sale support capability. We hired and worked to develop deep strategic sales and application engineering capabilities that enabled our involvement in early stages of client projects, positioning our uniquely tailored solutions ahead of the competitive bid stage process.

At PaR, our EoP became a clear and specialized area of focus in each business unit we established and developed, whether internally nurtured, acquired through partnering or, in many cases, by buying companies. We constantly reviewed our EoP elements to ensure improvement with a specialized focus as it related to the particular business unit. This business-specific focus added to a companywide perspective and fueled a significant and sustained profitability level for PaR, enabling continued investment in people, technology, and client-touch areas of our EoP.

As in any business, challenges and setbacks with lessons learned emerged in PaR, but a ceaseless focus on our business units' EoP aspects established a 20-year sustained run of improved and elevated performance. By comparison, as the Dow went from 11,000 in August 1999 to 2019's open at 23,346, increasing a Dow Index holder's value to $2.2 million if they invested $1 million, at PaR an investor over that period would achieve a return of *$20 million* for that same $1 million invested! More enduring, as leaders we saw so many people positively affected as well-paying, exciting jobs grew at a healthy pace at PaR and in our supply chain over our tenure together.

TUNING THE ENGINE

Because you are still reading, we know that not only did you survive a prolonged swim in several different pools, diving at various depths into these diverse experiences and descriptive examples, but that you also found the real-life examples beneficial and thought-provoking. We would now like to provide an outline of the key elements for your organization's EoP focus.

As we highlight the key EoP areas, it is critical to emphasize that leaders remain focused on financial elements vital for the organization's sustainability, while ensuring they bring three overarching dimensions to guide their EoP efforts:

- To be positively impacting
- To be growth-oriented
- To be a continuous-improvement-based organization

Certainly, few leaders would deny the necessity of continuous improvement of their services/products and business model. Businesses constantly strive to get ahead of the product lifecycle, from introduction to growth to maturity to decline—and to restart the cycle before decline settles in!). We prefer to think in multi-dimensional terms, recognizing that our response must always involve creative destruction as a multi-generational product-service-solution plan would dictate. Consider this diagram that illustrates this concept in simple terms.

Each product/service has a birth, then growth, and eventually a decline. We encourage you to think ahead of this creative destruction cycle and plan for it in your strategy, energizing a new cycle before decline settles into your customer's perceptions, your workplace culture, your competitive position, and your financial value.

What have you done to ensure the best efforts to incorporate EoP imperatives for your particular business into your POISED Strategy?

With this question as a launching point and the product/service cycle as a foundation, we present five key imperatives necessary for a finely tuned, optimal EoP that creates value holistically for the organization.

EoP Imperative 1: Strategic Actions for Consistent Investment in Profitable-Growth, Highest-Margin Capability

What are you doing today to identify areas for improvement, now and for the future? How are you tracking these efforts today through simple, useful metrics?

Most importantly, have you performed the difficult assessments to ensure that your most significant margin generators for today, and for tomorrow, have the best leadership leading development and improvement of the offerings so profit growth can fund the future?

Have you looked inside or, if necessary, outside the organization to be sure these best leaders are in place and being developed for the future?

For EoP success, you and your leadership team must think critically about and work diligently to implement these key aspects:

1. The organization's Strategy to win must clearly drive EoPs, with care that current and future highest-margin offerings represent a win for all constituents (internal and external).
2. For the identified EoP offerings, clients must experience clear differentiators. The organization must develop and

evolve these differentiated offerings through time investment, strategic and operational focus, and sustained financial investment in chosen priorities.

Significant margin-producing offerings are critical to generate ongoing income for investment in expanding the market success of today's and tomorrow's high-margin offerings. Your organizational strategy must make this path forward clear. Some strategic plans must honestly begin by admitting that the current situation is not sustainable. To recover, the organization may need to experience a defined period of negative or reduced bottom-line results to fund the creation of the next generation of high-margin profit generators. Worse long-term results could be waiting if the organization does not face the situation directly and make and communicate clear plans to the key constituents. While such a discussion and commitment can be very challenging, it may be necessary to avert sucking the team into an unrecoverable negative position.

A Strategy to win in the marketplace—and to continue to win with high-margin products that your organization can deliver—represents a key focus of the POISED Model's EoP component. *Have you made this winning Strategy central to your strategic plan to build on your organizational strengths?* Remember that a diligent implementation of the Strategy element (Chapter 4) sets your organization up for success, identifying key strategic actions, assigning resources for performance and accountability, and setting the organization in motion to complete the plan.

A Strategy to win in the marketplace—and to continue to win with high-margin products that your organization can deliver—represents a key focus of the POISED Model's EoP component.

In emphasis Number 2, we will discuss the area of learning from clients their most critical, urgent needs which help drive the prioritization of your EoP offerings. While a few companies, Apple being a great example in their early days, set out to create products people did not know they needed, we would argue that talking with clients, having deep relationships that enable true understanding and honest discussions, are the best way to discern what your particular clients need most and what they are willing to pay more to receive.

EoP Imperative 2: Leadership Constancy of Purpose to Sell and Deliver High-Margin Services and Products

What actions does the team take every day to ensure continued success of your strategically chosen high-margin offerings?

How are leaders creating an organizational focus on the high-margin offerings?

Further, we suggest additional action-driver questions to ask your team as you plan and operate to sell and deliver high-margin services and products.

What are your people doing in the marketplace to drive revenue? How are they selling, marketing, involving strategic partners, utilizing appropriate sales channels, and streamlining the sales and delivery process to meet client needs?

What are your people doing to design or redesign internal processes and tools—as well as involving the key people most knowledgeable in these processes—to achieve high-margin offering strategic goals in sales and delivery?

What are your team members and/or sales channel partners doing to deeply understand client needs today and tomorrow, and to recognize what clients are truly willing to pay for? What is your process for converting these learnings into development of the next generation of offerings? Do you have a multi-generation-planning process for your offerings?

What are your organization's product/service development actions and priorities?

The full expression of the actions arising from these questions requires technical, sales and marketing, financial, and other functional areas of expertise, integrated and working as a team, to define the individual actions to assess, improve, and grow the strategic plan's high-margin offerings.

Often, internal expertise to assess and then make the changes needed to prioritize the EoP-focused offerings, and sales of these offerings, has limitations based on historical decisions and gravity of the past. A fresh perspective offered by key hires, creative-disruptive team members, and external consultants and thought leaders—hand-chosen for their expertise and the task at hand—can be useful in shifting the organization away from "business as usual" to the open frontier of a promising potential future. Make sure this EoP imperative area gets the focus it deserves, proactively and continuously, and not after organizational momentum heads in a negative direction.

EoP Imperative 3: Maintain a Constant Cash Emphasis

How do leaders ensure positive cash flow?

How do they leverage available funds for reinvestment in the business?

How do leaders prioritize what areas of the business—such as R&D, learning and development, sales and marketing, technology, capital, etc.—in which to invest to drive current and future growth?

While EoP Imperative 2 assures that your business will continue to generate the profits needed, Imperative 3 assures that you have money in your bank account. With cash-on-hand as a daily priority, leadership should ensure stability and growth in key balance sheet items including Working Capital and Capital Structure to support the business' financial goals. To restate a well-worn, but vivid and illuminating expression: "You can't eat inventory." Even in the food business, while you literally may be able to eat inventory, it is never a practical way to pay suppliers and employees! Cash is king (or queen) for a viable business.

While financially oriented team members in your organization will consider this balance sheet focus old-hat, it is important that all leadership team members and others at all levels of the organization become aware of and focus on ways they can affect cash positively. Clearly defined and articulated metrics become key; sharing these at the relevant meetings and in appropriate communications mediums for employees takes on a higher priority when leaders prioritize cash balance sheet strength.

> Leadership team members and others at all levels of the organization must become aware of and focus on ways they can affect cash positively.

Organizations must hyper-focus on Working Capital, which is key to sustaining cash reserves and maintaining a positive cash flow. Working Capital includes Inventory and Accounts Receivable (what clients owe you, which is important for large clients and very important on a total client basis, as is the average age of Accounts Receivable). Specific businesses may have other huge areas of Working Capital such as costs in goods and services that are considered "work-in-progress" (WIP), or "unbilled" but completed work/recorded revenue. While accounting folks all train in and manage Working Capital, area(s) of highest impact may vary from business to business.

Typically, Capital Structure is an area reserved for the CFO and the CEO or most senior-level people involved in the organization's banking and/or investing arena. As a leader wanting to invest, take time to understand your Capital Structure, your business' cost of capital, and the timing of debt payments to support your planning. Your organization also should have a contingency plan for access to additional funding (lines of credit or other resource pools) should it be required.

This chapter's intent is not to drag you through a financial deep-dive but to ensure a leadership-level awareness of critical EoP areas, so the details beyond this high-level introduction are left as subjects for a different discussion. Ensuring you, the leader, are tied into the financial expertise in your organization, and assuring financial leaders have a strong and active voice in your leadership strategies, plans, and actions, is a critical organizational message we want to emphasize.

EoP Imperative 4: Hyper-Focus on Client-Facing and Internal Costs

Is your organization's leadership team constantly focused on keeping a lean structure and lean expenditure mindset?

Has cost structure and profitability of each business unit been re-evaluated recently to ascertain if it is efficient today?

Are team members motivated to work efficiently and rewarded for generating cost savings?

Even when funding of growth and high-margin offerings development and sales succeeds, a lean small company mindset is valuable and needed. If there is a constant focus in this area, along with an agile culture that responds well to unforeseen developments, a cost-conscious emphasis will bear fruit in times of austerity—and even more in times of growth because higher net profits enable flexibility for further strategic investment.

Work processes, from new service/product development through client delivery, require routine and systematic evaluation and improvement to root out causes of variability that waste time, money, and resources. A progressive organization empowers all levels of the workforce to understand the processes in which they work, to surface opportunities for incremental improvement and innovation, and to engage team members in creating positive change. Organizations typically lose more than they gain when they try to "cut their way to success", so ensure the message and the rewards target cost optimization and effectiveness.

> A progressive organization empowers all levels of the workforce to understand the processes in which they work, to surface opportunities for incremental improvement and innovation, and to engage team members in creating positive change.

Engaging the supply chain in cost optimization offers an additional opportunity to keep a lean expenditure mindset at the forefront. Some organizations use their procurement scale as a power dynamic to strong-arm suppliers into lower costs; better organizations invite supplier-partners into the product-service development and delivery cycle to find ways to optimize cost. While the strong-arm scale approach may work short-term to reduce materials and supplies cost, long-term partnering produces a constructive, often innovative commitment to whole lifecycle cost.

Without doubt, cost-effective operation bolsters the bottom line. However your organization drives this imperative through your EoP, ensure the focus remains on lean operation as a positive profit multiplier without becoming a culture and relationship detractor.

EoP Imperative 5: Relevant and Clear Performance Metric Reporting

Who is responsible for each strategic EoP priority?
How are they and the organization measuring the critical EoP elements?
Have the right areas of focus been identified or is more work needed?

Monitoring, reporting, analyzing, and acting on key metrics that drive awareness and continued improvements in business-specific EoP areas must be led by senior leaders. And, making the metrics relevant and clear undoubtedly will require that senior leaders assist the individual functional areas in defining a manageable number of metrics—a "dashboard-style" set of metrics that produce much more value than the amount of effort needed to compile and to report the metrics.

At the right time, every organization also needs to consider how best to automate the key metrics to minimize performance monitoring effort and also to make the metrics visible to all key constituents. From the outset, do not let automation or the means by which metrics are reported—an Excel template with consistently formatted run/trend charts will do—delay or distract senior leaders or the functional teams in developing the metric set.

In fact, "manual" performance measurement compilation and analysis may serve to enhance ownership in and commitment to early performance measurement activities. Team members often feel a greater sense of pride in favorable performance, and accountability for unfavorable results, with their hands on the steering wheel. Post updated charts on a bulletin board, routinely share them in town hall meetings and employee forums and invite and encourage dialogue.

In developing your performance measurement and monitoring system, ask these questions routinely:

- Do you have an online real-time dashboard; a daily dashboard; or one that is utilized during weekly Fuel Meetings at every level?
- Does your factory/production team have daily/hourly/weekly/monthly metric(s)? What about Service? Sales? Product Management and Business Unit leadership?

- Are high-margin products, cash, and the balance sheet receiving sufficient attention through the metrics?

Ensure that the metrics you develop have clear operational definitions; that is, develop a concise statement clarifying the measure's EoP area and owner, units of measure, and time period for the measurement. A well-designed graphic display will include the performance trend over time, x/y axis labeling, a target-goal threshold, and an indicator to depict favorable performance (e.g., UP ⇧ is GOOD). More mature metric displays may incorporate upper and lower control limits, best competitor and/or best-in-class comparative data benchmarks, and a brief trend analysis summary.

Analysis, action, and improvement are key to a vibrant performance measurement system. Senior leaders should lead by example and engage the EoP business area leadership and teams to take action on performance measurement findings, driving sustained performance or turning around unfavorable performance.

To repeat an oft-uttered management quote, "In God we trust; all others bring data!" Your EoP measurement system helps create a culture of management by fact, sending a message that leaders will require all levels of the organization to measure and analyze the organization's performance and follow-up appropriately. While reinforcing accountability and responsibility for performance, the organization's performance assessment, analysis, and action should support strategic and operational alignment, intelligent decision-making, learning and improvement, and recognition . . . and not punitive action.

SUSTAINING THE ENGINE

Take a moment and imagine the ceaseless rotational energy clicking in your ear and in your mind if you are standing by an old

Harris printing press as sheets feed into the cylinder section, receiving indelible ink and forming an imprint on sheet after sheet after sheet, at 4,000 to 18,000 sheets per hour[11]. Then, make your drive to create a relentless, enduring focus on a solid EoP match this unstoppable machine!

With the sound of the mechanical consistency ringing in your ears as a conscious driver of focus on your specific EoP, you will position your team and organization for exceptional results and sustained, elevated performance. To accomplish this objective, POISED ensures sustainability and elevated performance by never letting you lose sight of what it takes to fuel profit to fund organizational growth and success.

Creating an operational rhythm—a consistent cadence of monitoring, analysis, action, and communication—requires diligence and dedication. Be consistent but also build your monitoring system so it may respond to rapid or unexpected organizational or external changes and provide timely data (as Chapter 3 reminds us: Identify priorities, especially emerging imperatives). If the marketplace shifts and responding makes strategic sense, so should your performance measurement and management system. Embedding learning and improvement as organizational drivers makes your organization stronger.

Whether you are leading in the restaurant business, at one of today's modern printing or manufacturing companies, in an automation hardware/software or other high-tech business, a ministry, a service organization, a school, or any of an almost infinite number of other teams of resources focused on a mission, you must do your part to ensure a focus on sustainability and elevating performance. With your hands on the wheel of the EoP, you can drive performance to your desired destination.

This chapter provides thoughts and summarizes actions to help you create an enduring, urgent emphasis on the POISED EoP remaining in place long after you have completed your leadership assignment or moved on to the next challenge.

Our experience with strong leaders is they want to do more—they want to excel, grow, sustain excellence, and create a legacy of opportunity for the next generation of leaders. This means they will focus on making all facets of POISED strong and operational with an understanding and appropriate emphasis on the EoP to ensure the rhythm of performance improvement continues today, tomorrow, and into the future.

Next, Chapter 6 will tie the entire POISED Model together as "the rubber hits the road." We will focus on Do: what you do on a regular basis to make a difference and add value at the highest level.

POISED® Key Points Summary	
People	Develop each person to their fullest capability and enable optimal utilization of their Strengths
Octane	. . . of the organization – Mission, Vision, Values (MV^2) – and results driven, shaped through continuous improvement in all facets of the organization
Identify	. . . all priorities, challenges, opportunities, and metrics – to act with wise use of resources
Strategy	. . . to leverage Strengths to win for all facets of the organization, clearly communicated to all constituencies and acted upon
Engine of Profitability	. . . to fund growth supporting the Strategy to win
Do	
POISED® Integrated Model	

6

DO

*"Execution has to be a part of a company's strategy
and its goals. It is the missing link between aspirations
and results. As such, it is a major—indeed,
the major—job of a business leader."*
–Larry Bossidy, Acclaimed CEO and author of *Execution*–

Decide and then Do! As you navigate through the P, O, I, S, and E elements of the POISED Model, you and your team make decisions and established priorities. You reaffirm or reimagine your Mission, Vision, Values (MV^2) and you make commitments for how you will build on the strengths of your People. You select high-leverage goals to pursue a growth-oriented, high-profit Strategy and you define key metrics in your EoP for monitoring and driving performance. Your decisions elevate the key actions you will Do, as well as what you chose to abandon or NOT to Do.

Now, the POISED Model comes down to work—the work of applying resources (financial, people, materials, etc.) to chosen activities (Strategy, goals, action plans) to produce the results that your organization, your customers, your team members, and your stakeholders deserve and expect. The whole organization must put their full force behind (and in front of!) Strategy achievement, engaging and improving planning, sales, delivery, and support processes to make it happen.

As you take action and Do, you must align and make your plans, processes, measures, and actions consistent. Unify your team members by articulating a compelling Vision and Strategy, set up performance management structures to reinforce action, monitor and make adjustments . . . and then keep your eye and hands on the ball to make sure it gets over the goal line.

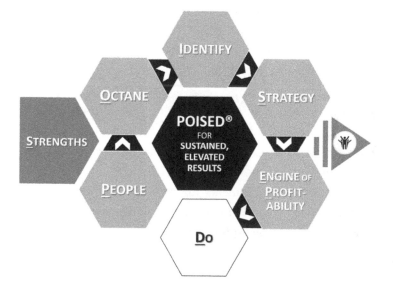

LEADERSHIP STORY

Mark's friend John Peterson won a silver medal at the 1972 Summer Olympics in Munich, Germany, in the 82-kg weight class, the same year Dan Gable of wrestling fame and John's brother, Ben, won gold medals.

Then, in the year before the 1976 Olympics, John suffered a serious shoulder injury, acquired mononucleosis, stayed in the hospital for 5 days, and then developed a serious infection on his knee, an incredibly critical part of the body necessary to perform even the most basic wrestling moves. How was John even going to try out again for the Olympics, let alone win a spot and compete for a medal in Montreal in 1976?

In real anguish I (Mark) have listened to John recount his serious health challenges in 1975 and 1976. His painful, repetitive, shoulder rehabilitation began four times per day and continued eventually at lesser frequency over many months, allowing him to avoid a recommended surgery that would have prevented him from competing.

After improving his shoulder strength, John traveled to Russia to compete against many of the world's best wrestlers. He came back exhausted, drained, without any energy and, with a visit to the hospital, John was kept there to rehydrate and recover from mononucleosis. Not long after his discharge, John developed a terrible knee infection that furthered the list of health obstacles that would have prevented most mortals and many elite athletes from even considering an Olympics bid, especially in such an all-in competitive event such as wrestling that demands incredible physical strength and stamina.

With a strong work ethic and an amazing ability to overcome insurmountable odds, John did make it through the 1976 U.S. Olympics trials and made the team. Talking with John, I specifically wanted to know, "What did you Do to prepare for the possibility of competing at the highest level?" His response demonstrated his unwavering conviction to compete.

As you can imagine, preparation for wrestling in the Olympics was incredible. John described his three arduous workouts per day, essentially every day over weeks and months. Factoring in his injuries and illness, John's ability to prepare became of utmost importance, not unlike what a business leader sees is necessary to prepare because of com-

petition, unforeseeable circumstances, industry shocks, resource shortages, wars or pandemics that shake the world, and so many other conditions we used to call "black swans" but seem to occur frequently today.

John's journey reminds me that three aspects are essential in preparing a wrestler's body and mind for the arduous sport:

1. Learning: Practice technique and skills to enable executing at the highest level. Get critiqued by people like Dan Gable, Ben Peterson, and other elite coaches and athletes in the sport. John was unafraid to mix-up the routine while assuring the goal of getting better, in conditioning and wrestling technique, was driven personally and steadily over time.

2.   Conditioning: Build and sustain strength and cardiovascular capacities. Weight training for strength and for endurance (fast- and slow-twitch muscles), running, and other "cardio" workouts such as a little basketball. In John's case, all of this mixed with hard work on the farm and some construction jobs.

3.   Wrestling: Wrestle a great variety of wrestlers. For instance, John chose some stronger, some lighter and faster, those in other countries with different techniques, and many more to test and to elevate his capabilities.

As he recounted to me, John will humbly tell you about the intensity of physical preparation and discipline at any level of detail that you want. John also will share about his mental preparation, which we will discuss a bit more later in the chapter.

We often think of wrestling as a solo individual sport. In one sense, an Olympic wrestler has no one else to point to when they lose a match, so it is individual. However, winning for the team and for national pride makes it much more than an individual sport. No world-class wrestler has ever succeeded without a team of people preparing them over the years, and sparring with them, training them, and teaching them.

For example, Bill Farrell, the 1972 Olympic Coach, who knew the Russian approach to wrestling, and Jim Peckham, who observed John's over-focus on one takedown technique (double-leg takedowns), provided John with strategic inputs about his wrestling decisions. Dan Gable emphasized conditioning and competition and he and others simply wrestled with John. Wayne Baughman, 1976 Olympic Coach, taught technique. Knowing through John's experience that Olympic wrestling success takes a team is a contextual lesson from which we thankfully borrow.

In this chapter emphasizing your leadership actions, what you Do is vitally important to be POISED for results and sustained, elevated performance in an organization where people love working and contributing. But, know that you are not alone. Like John, you must surround yourself with a team of strong and knowledgeable performers.

John's emphasis on Learning, Conditioning, and Wrestling (Doing) the actual work is informative as we illustrate the importance of what *you* Do. We have written about being a Continuous Learning Organization (coined by Peter Senge) in Chapter 2, Octane. If this continuous learning emphasis weakens, despite a business performing ahead of its competition, other competitors that grow and learn more quickly will surpass you. Conditioning, or training to get stronger in every element of the business constantly, is part of assuring your learning can be put to work effectively. Finally, wrestle . . . Engage . . . and Do! The Fuel Meetings (see meeting agenda in the Appendix) assure all critical elements are addressed every week and everyone has their opportunity to surface and address current, relevant, real needs and issues. These steps ensure steady engagement in the business environment in which you work.

The rubber really hits the road in what we Do as leaders. This effort is how we fulfill the POISED Model elements and how we ensure the rhythm of the business fuels the employees to be truly engaged—because they enjoy their work and the people around them; they align with the mission, the vision, and the values; and the organization enables them to go all-out to satisfy clients and to enable the business to succeed and thrive.

DOING THE WORK

Think about the tools and structure of this chapter like organizing your calendar around the things you know are important to Do. As is often said, do a calendar check: if you say it is important, then it should be on your calendar.

Are you really doing what you say is important?

If it is not reflected on your calendar, you really must question your commitment. Leaders demonstrating priorities (what the team sees YOU do and then what THEY participate in) represents a key source of Octane for the business. Model the way forward through your communication, your behaviors, and your actions.

The POISED Do approach includes five imperatives to successful implementation, detailed below with a framework you can model and adapt to your organization's and teams' needs.

Do Imperative 1: Cultivate an Operational Rhythm

Leaders must ensure a rhythm of thoughtful and productive daily, weekly, monthly, quarterly, and annual actions by the whole team and follow-up focused on elevating the entire organization. In brief, these essentials include:

- Maintaining a daily rhythm of customer, employee, continuous improvement engagement
- Assuring weekly Fuel Meetings
- Reporting performance in the metric scoreboard at least monthly
- Holding quarterly sessions to return to commitments
- Resetting Strategic, Financial, and HR Plans annually

Daily Rhythm. We ask you to consider several key questions as you lead the rhythm of your day-to-day business; your responses and actions demonstrate your dedication to build and to enable a workplace that enables high performance.

How are you engaging leaders and fueling Octane?

How are you assuring client-focused delivery excellence aimed at engaging all elements of the POISED Model?

Does fulfilling your mission receive priority in your Fuel Meetings, metrics, and coaching conversations?

How do you lead to create and drive an open culture? Are you assuring regular time for open discussion of business/people/organizational issues so the problems are tackled and owners follow up? Do you make sure that people expect to truly address business issues regularly when they arise?

When there are issues, are you personally making sure the real root causes are discussed, people's strengths are employed, and resolution paths are committed to by engaged leaders?

Taking action to address these questions will help you create a culture where leaders expect a high degree of openness and are leaning into and openly leveraging the People/high-Octane culture you want to establish for sustained, elevated performance. Remember, good issue discussion, or as we call it "Positive Conflict," always goes back to the formula of $MV^2 + I^2$ (Positive Conflict centers on Mission, Vision, Values + Issues and Ideas).

> Leaders must ensure a rhythm of thoughtful and productive daily, weekly, monthly, quarterly, and annual actions by the whole team and followup focused on elevating the entire organization.

Weekly-Monthly-Quarterly Rhythm. The weekly, monthly, and quarterly rhythm kicks off accountability, communication, and follow-up of the organization's strategic goals. The weekly rhythm starts the ball rolling and includes consistent use of the DBS tool and approach to build momentum at all levels in the organization. Key components of the rhythm include:

- Weekly Fuel Meetings must include a rigorous and crisp schedule for accomplishing critical needs. The following is a framework for the weekly Fuel Meeting:
  a. Ice breaker/personal sharing to start the meeting and get people engaged in a team mindset—share strengths, personal items, "values moments", etc.
  b. Metrics highlighting the most important identified aspects of the business and whether they are on or off track, with ownership
  c. Client/Employee/Market/Competitive highlights
  d. Follow-up on weekly and quarterly 90-day goals and strategic priorities
  e. DBS items
- Weekly or bi-weekly one-on-one discussions with all direct reports/key leaders including:
  a. Mentoring to address individual- and business-specific needs
  b. Staying close to real business opportunities and issues
  c. Discussing and ensuring progress on, and identifying obstacles around, that leader's 90-day goals and commitments
  d. Discussing critical market and internal aspects related to the mission and vision

We like asking the direct report/key leader to come to these sessions with their agenda to ensure their concerns, challenges, and needs are discussed. We complete the meeting by including items we know to be a priority that were not on the initial agenda.

- Monthly meetings—tracking against commitments through a rhythm of measuring and adjusting, and focusing on financial and Strategic priorities and major 90-day goals

- Quarterly meetings—revisiting and redirecting (as needed) 90-day goal setting/measuring
- Annual planning—a significant milestone for assessing performance and refining (or reinventing) plans that includes:

  a. *Financial Monitoring.* Following annual planning, in addition to weekly financial metrics at the Fuel Meeting, monthly results reporting will enable timely analysis and learning with associated adjustments. Annual planning should engage critical thinking and have a results focus to ensure a fresh look with POISED elements, especially EoP, in the plan. It is critical to engage the entire senior leadership team in developing the financial plans and managing actions that can help regularly produce good results. A good financial leader working with individual team members, and then supported by other leaders when finalizing the total plan as a team for buy-in by all, can solidify the commitment as challenging plans are developed and implemented.

  b. *Strategic Plan Review and Adjustment.* As emphasized in the POISED Strategy element, developing the Strategic Plan as a team, communicating appropriately to all constituents, and quarterly follow-up are essential. Embedding critical actions into the weekly Fuel Meetings, with accountability, keeps the plans in front of the team and enables a steady focus to accomplish significant strategic steps for the business.

c. *Strategic HR Planning.* A Strategic Plan that does not incorporate a Strategic HR Plan misses the key ingredient for success: People! A comprehensive HR planning process incorporating, at a minimum, annual goals, assessments, coaching-mentoring, and succession, can make a tremendous difference in the pace at which an organization can grow its capacity. Then, living the HR action plans in partnership with each team member throughout the year is integral to a learning, growing organization. Annual Strategic HR sessions, driven and guided by the overall Strategy, will influence daily, weekly, monthly, and quarterly learning and actions and should include:

   i.   Transformational aspects needed for the longer term—changes needed to build and to nurture a high-performance culture.

   ii. People development—within a routine development and succession approach, leaders should ensure increased emphasis at appropriate times for different aspects of the organization (such as talent acquisition to fill key gaps or learning and development to develop needed competencies for strategic success). Leaders at all levels and across the organization should be provided the opportunity to give input to peers and offer cross-functional perspectives that the direct manager never sees. Other specific People development actions are outlined in Chapter 2 and serve as a good reminder for annual Strategic HR Planning.

   iii. Succession planning—consider retirements or departures that may occur, identify backups for critical roles, and plan for needed organizational changes to achieve strategic objectives. These succession plans convert to clear action plans that can involve training and developmental assignments, hiring plans that need leadership and execution, coaching, and other action-oriented critical thoughts, all with follow-up by senior leadership and HR working together.

iv. Individual HR priorities—these must become a set of actions aligned to organizational goals, embodied in a living action plan implemented each week and throughout the year, led by a strategic HR person supporting all leaders.

Done well, an effectively facilitated, open yet confidential, annual senior team strategic HR discussion can be immensely meaningful and productive. Leaders should adopt a systematic approach such as using the "nine-box" (see Appendix) or other talent management resource to ensure a cross-functional team review of all key employees that most impact the direction of the business and to ensure the organization remains strong while fulfilling new needs architected in the Strategic Plan. As this process becomes a core part of what an organization does, every employee can be elevated as formal and informal leaders make development an integral part of daily interactions.

We have described the weekly resource, the Fuel Meeting (see Appendix), which is essential for ensuring discipline and productive accountability, but also for keeping the fuel, the octane of the organization, at the highest level possible. Communication, trust, accountability, and constructive disagreements are essential to a high-performing team. Adopting a rhythm of using the business challenge resolution process, the DBS Tool (see Appendix), and a mindset to always address business needs directly and gain the benefit of everyone's strengths and experience, also are key to motivating performance and assuring sustained excellence.

> We fully embrace the old maxim, "what you do speaks so loudly, I cannot hear what you are saying," in the Do element of POISED. Leaders model the way forward through their behaviors and actions.

Timely recognition of the need to address identified priority challenges and opportunities, leveraging the strengths of those who see these opportunities most clearly, can truly energize the team, help avoid the untenable stress we discussed in Chapter 2 (see the Yerkes-Dodson law diagram), and enable you and your team to create the environment of "optimal stress" for all-employee engagement and for producing results.

We fully embrace the old maxim, "what you do speaks so loudly, I cannot hear what you are saying," in the Do element of POISED. Every day (EVERY day), an organization must live the values, led by senior leaders, of Building Trust, Enabling Positive Conflict, Demonstrating True Commitment, and Practicing Accountability. These are essentials. No one is perfect, but the ability to acknowledge, learn, and move on is all-important to nurture over time. This commitment will fortify your approach to achieve the desired team results and outcomes for which you planned . . . and much more.

Do Imperative 2: Focus on Mission, Vision, and Values (MV²) as the Driving Force

The POISED Octane key element is not simply a nice concept using a quirky leadership word. In our experience, leaders who elevate organizational performance demonstrate they live the Values and they always keep the Mission and Vision in view. Employees see whether you are leading and walking the walk of the Values and focusing on the Mission, not just on numbers or your own personal success.

Living the above Values can help you discern when short-term actions harm the opportunity to achieve the Vision and enable you to make corrections. Demonstrating MV² alignment through actions has a huge impact. Ensuring the leaders you select, as well as the rest of the team, all are aligned on the same Mission and Vision, and share the same Values, will determine your level of success at accomplishing your POISED objectives.

Assuring your actions and the leadership team's actions remain consistent to MV² is essential. At the same time, we know from decades of experience, that we will all fall down in our responsibility in this area. We need to listen and to hear the feedback when this happens, respond honestly, and work to get back on track. This honesty and integrity, as well as what Thrall, McNicol and McElrath, in *The Ascent of a Leader*, call, "an environment of grace" needed to allow openness and to learn quickly from mistakes, is ever-important in maintaining high engagement[12].

Do Imperative 3: Walk the Talk as Leaders

What each leader does and *how* they do it either builds and maintains highest Octane in the team or drags the team down. We ask you to keep these questions in mind to help you organize your activities and priorities and where you choose to focus in your Fuel Meetings and other interactions with your team:

How are you holding your leaders, including yourself, accountable to MV² consistency?

How is the leadership team remaining focused on their Strategic Plan commitments?

Are leaders showing up to the Fuel Meetings prepared and energized to support the team? Are leaders demonstrating honesty in their conversations and accountability and an action-orientation? Are you openly guiding them to do this if you see someone not engaged?

How are you assisting your leaders in choosing the best leaders to be in your organization? How can you become more engaged with guiding HR in this effort, and is this a part of your strategic HR process yet? Are your leaders using the AEF (Alignment-Engagement-Fit) resource as they assess their team members for optimal fulfillment of their roles (see Appendix)?

How are you celebrating, informing, announcing, engaging employees, and leadership teams in big events such as capitalization, merger/acquisition, major competitive wins, significant financial achievements, and other major change and milestone situations? Engage your HR team and others with strong interpersonal strengths to help ensure these opportunities for highlighting the big events are not missed.

When "life or death" business situations occur (such as a cash crisis, other major overarching considerations such as extreme HR issues, a pandemic-driven abrupt slowdown, etc.), maximizing Octane by keeping a Mission and Vision focus and doubling down on living your shared Values will help you and your team navigate problem-solving, communication, and resolution of the crisis. When the solution effort seems overwhelming, bolster your business momentum with targeted Fuel Meetings and do not lose sight of the identified priorities.

Make sure you give thought to ensuring proper communication, understanding some aspects must remain confidential, and engage your partners with the strengths that balance your natural strengths. Balance the need for candor, as well as confidentiality when called for, and exercise your strengths to remain a steady leader while under fire in crisis situations. From our past experiences in surviving crisis situations, we cannot overstate the importance of keeping the Octane-driving Mission and Vision focus and team strengths utilization in mind during crisis times, knowing that we will never act perfectly in all circumstances. We know that maintaining respectful relationships with people, ensuring open and frequent communication, having strong and trusting relationships, and feeding the Octane of the team are all crucial to get through challenging times.

 Maintaining respectful relationships with people, ensuring open and frequent communication, having strong and trusting relationships, and feeding the Octane of the team are all crucial to getting through challenging times.

Supporting a strong people-development-focused HR culture, here are Octane-related practices for you to consider:

- *All-employee meetings (or Town Halls).* Maintain a rhythm of hosting all-employee meetings quarterly, or on another more frequent cycle if your situation allows. Help guide these communication sessions, calling on formal or informal leaders for major roles, and ensure the meetings are designed to cultivate energy around client successes, sales or marketing initiatives, continuous improvement opportunities and innovation, and business team successes. To the maximum extent possible, openly share financial results vs. plan in a constructive manner, helping to keep the team reality-focused and success-oriented.

- *Roundtables.* You and your senior leadership team should plan and hold roundtable meetings monthly, or more frequently, with the intent of real and open two-way communication. Utilize methods to truly engage the participants (we recommend cross-functional teams of 8 to 10 people representing nearly all of the functions and business/sales organizations). Often, such roundtable meetings are best held with an HR partner and the senior leader together.

    a. In these cross-functional sessions, when leaders enable each participant to communicate openly, people can establish deeper knowledge of and relationships with colleagues with whom they do not always work.

    b. As the leader, come prepared to give an encouraging, appropriate and thoughtful, crisp business update, helping employees get a good feel for the business pulse.

    c. You or your HR lead should facilitate cross-functional discussions during these informal sessions. Ask all participants to come prepared to ask a question or to summarize an important success or issue in the business.

    d. Challenge yourself to learn something from every team member who participates and then communicate what you have gained in an engaging and productive manner.

    e. Practice a 24-hour rule of publishing brief, thoughtful notes or "speaking points" to encourage and inform those not present.

    f. At one business Mark led, introducing roundtable meetings had an impact on accelerating the Octane change in a series of ways. Larry, who Mark learned was one of the smartest guys in a shop that produced complex first-of-a-kind robotics, refused to attend the first roundtable until the HR leader insisted (Larry had no time for meetings, just getting work done). During the first extremely candid roundtable, everyone was highly encouraged to be open about issues they saw. Larry was the most candid. Mark and the HR leader emphasized the expectation that employees could bring up any issue, but they must also participate in identifying a solution direction. This began to plant the seed for accountability for improvement vs. griping. Within a few meetings, the tone went from a gripe session to a real cross-functional and action-oriented roundtable communication. Over time, this expectation became clear throughout the organization and people came prepared with issues and thoughts about improvements, as well as reports on successes already in progress. About this time, new supervisors were chosen in the shop. Larry, who initially seemed like the least cooperative team member, became the first supervisor chosen and one of the most impactful team leaders in the company. Already respected by the shop team who valued his knowledge, Larry demonstrated that, once allowed to contribute to improving the company, he was immensely motivated to advance the organization. Larry later became THE advocate for shop employees taking ownership of safety and, ultimately, influenced the entire company.

- *Lunch-and-Learns.* Casual learning sessions with internal and external facilitators/presenters support knowledge sharing in a learning organization. Make sure someone on your team takes the lead so you have a regular rhythm of inviting folks internally, or suppliers/other external partners, to sponsor a lunch or virtual gathering that provides employees with useful information related to the business. For instance, great suppliers love to educate their clients with the hope of ensuring business. Done well and managed, these lunch-and-learn meetings are great tools for a learning organization.

- *Celebrations and Rewards and Recognition.* How do you and your team, and the broader organization, celebrate successes in an appropriate manner? Ask HR to help each group think about what, and how, to do this. An approach at the organization level that balances a formalized recognition framework with ease of use can help to reinforce a cultural expectation of recognition. Use recognition to strengthen the fabric of the team and, at the individual level, get to know how each individual prefers to be recognized. Leverage MV^2 as an aligning force, recognizing and celebrating accomplishments and actions that reflect these guiding organizational elements.

- *Employee Health Improvement.* It should not surprise you that employees bring their personal lives to work. Approaches to support team members as they navigate life's challenges—familial, financial, mental and physical health, etc.—support a healthy and caring workplace where people can give their all. Here are two ideas:

    a. Once challenged to review an interesting Harvard health study (it concluded better health came down to doing four things well: better eating, better exercise routine, no smoking, and weight management), our HR leader developed an efficient and high-visibility

Health Encouragement Plan. Each quarter, employees signed up to the "4 for 4 Plan", with just a few guidelines for self-monitoring. The program included modest $25 incentives per employee when 25% of employees in that location achieved "4 for 4" status that quarter; if 50% succeed that quarter, the incentive rose to $50 for each employee, and so on up to $100 per employee.

b. Our HR leader also established a new Health Screen program, bringing in an expert health screen company. The company scheduled a few days each year onsite to take blood work and record other health parameters from all employees who signed up. Due to its demonstrated health improvement benefits, and associated health insurance savings, neither employees nor the company paid for this service— the screening company was paid by the insurance company through lower costs they incur. However, the most meaningful and fulfilling results from this program came for a small number of people who received emergency calls from the health provider and caught severe health issues as a result of the screen, literally saving some employees' lives in their view. The annual screen was often accompanied by actual hugs from employees to the HR leader because of the life-saving impact.

Do Imperative 4: Ensure Presence and Engagement as Leaders

Leaders set the tone for the organization through their actions, not their words. Remember this quote: "If you see me doing it, then it's

OK for you to do it." Employees model the behaviors they see from their leaders (good or bad!).

As organizations grow, and the CEO and other senior leaders have helped develop their teams, engagement of employees and client intimacy will be even greater across the organization and at all levels of leadership, from front line to executive.

Great leaders are present. They work directly with the delivery and sales teams. They work with the functional leaders. They engage with the support process leaders. They expect the leaders of these teams, and the individuals on the teams, to work together. This should be part of the fabric of the organization. As organizations grow, and the CEO and other senior leaders have helped develop their teams, engagement of employees and client intimacy will be even greater across the organization and at all levels of leadership, from front line to executive. Remember, leadership is a *contact* sport!

The CEO or business leader's presence with senior leaders, clients, and employees is critical. Be prepared. Listen to learn, not to respond. Fulfill the role of a Transformational Leader, internally and externally. Incorporate strengths, find ways to engage leaders, and help them engage their teams so everyone in the organization can work in their sweet spot (strengths appropriate), where they enjoy pushing themselves to accomplish the mission daily. Challenge people to grow, to lead, to execute, and to remain focused on clients, quality, efficiency, and continuous improvement. Leadership presence is vital for total success in the organization!

Do Imperative 5: Demonstrate Dedication to the POISED Elements and Agility

Leaders must be flexible and open to corrections that lead to improvement and growth—as individuals, for the team, and for the entire business. Leaders must demonstrate their Do commitment to the organization by actions that support the POISED business model:

- **People.** Leaders Do by setting the example for how to deal with people and how to make thoughtful people decisions—honestly, professionally, and respectfully; caring for their development and their learning; with a focus on hiring leaders who have requisite skills, strengths, and capabilities and who also bring a passion for consistent MV^2 focus.

- **Octane.** What Leaders Do drives Octane—not just in the obvious and positive aspects, but also in how they deal with difficulties, how they lead in challenging times, and how they develop their teams. What leaders Do daily, weekly, and over time creates reality, authenticity, and decisiveness and enables engagement at all levels in the organization.

- **Identify.** Visionary leaders Do the hard work of envisioning the future—motivating improvement in all that the business and its leaders Do, including clarifying what is measured, simplifying key metric tracking, and acting on analysis findings. Leaders must drive accountability for metric performance and report on strategic priorities and priority improvement actions and help ensure the team is identifying and assuring resolution through DBS (Driving Business Solutions) of all priority business challenges (see Appendix).

- **Strategy.** By translating long-range future plans into implementable, short-term action plans, leaders articulate and generate a clear, crisp Strategy—leveraging the organization's strengths, communicating priorities and progress, leading buy-in by all and, most importantly, implementing the Strategy.

- **EoP.** An organization without a strong and growing financial foundation cannot survive, and leaders must drive high-profit service/product delivery and business model optimization—passionately, consistently keeping the organization attuned to and laser-focused on the keys to the profitability engine each day, each week, and over time.

- **Do.** Leaders set the tone at the top of the organization. What they Do (or do NOT Do) communicates more directly than any slogan, memo, announcement, or exhortation. Demonstrate constancy of purpose and champion the effort. Model the best behaviors and actions you want others to adopt—and then accept nothing less than their best.

FUELING WHAT YOU DO

As we summarize key aspects that illuminate the importance of what leaders Do, we ask you to think about the leaders who ensure the rhythm in your business.

Are you the only leader ensuring the rhythm in the business?

Do you have Driver Strengths? Do you have Responsibility as a Strength?

Does someone on your team have Consistency as a Strength (see CliftonStrengths Eight Categories in the Appendix)?

As you think through these questions, look for an opportunity to engage people who may excel at these activities in your organization based on their strengths and their opportunities for growth. It is wise to give deep consideration about who will ensure the success of the Do elements. Here are some thoughts we ask you to consider in implementing roles for Do:

- Are you leading the all-important weekly Fuel Meeting, or is your CFO or HR leader, or a COO-like person, better at this than you? What is your role in ensuring accountability and that the Octane elements occur weekly?

- Is Finance leading the weekly communication of financial metrics and the monthly financial close and communication process, such that all leaders are informed and up-to-date weekly and through clear reporting monthly? While many organizations are migrating to online financial metrics, we emphasize the importance of the CFO or other Finance functional leader communicating personally to a leadership team in-person or on a leadership team call.

- Are all leaders on board with their drumbeat of metrics reporting? Have they done the work to identify, define, and simplify the metrics, then prioritize and act on improvement areas, in their scopes of responsibility? How can you encourage this never-ending process of improving and targeting meaningful metrics?

- Who leads the quarterly accountability and 90-day goal-setting sessions?

- Is a Marketing or Business Development leader leading the Annual Strategy session or does that leader have a partner who will drive the process?

- Is HR leading, with ownership by all senior leaders, the candid and confidential annual Strategic HR planning process? Is there regular and high-quality follow-up on the plans developed in these sessions to ensure a living process of real individual development across the organization?

- Are all leaders dedicated to setting a daily example of fueling Octane through:

a. Living the values, and even reminding each other when needed?

b. Assuring client and quality focus?

c. Driving to fulfill the Mission and aiming at the Vision?

d. Demonstrating accountability, accepting responsibility for not being perfect, and modeling continuous learning?

e. Communicating openly from a basis of reality and authenticity?

We encourage you to work through these questions and emphasize habitual, disciplined use of the POISED tools (see Appendix) as you work to grow your people resources, model and teach the behaviors that sustain results, and ensure MV^2 alignment in everything you Do.

So, now that we have outlined key practices and learnings for the Do element of POISED, let us return to the beginning of the chapter and revisit our wrestler friend, John Peterson.

If you travel to Comstock, Wisconsin, a dairy farm town of 754 people just outside of Cumberland, you will see a sign in town that the family and friends of John and Ben Peterson erected. It has a wrestling action picture carved into the large wooden sign and simply says:

Ben Peterson—1972: Gold, 1976: Silver
John Peterson—1972 Silver, 1976: Gold

Yes, John won a gold in 1976 despite all the obstacles stacked up against this possibility! John's preparation paid off: improving mentally and physically; focusing on his mission; planning what was needed and learning from the best; doing what was needed daily, weekly, and at competitions; and, finally, executing on what he had prepared to Do. As John explained, concentrating on and taking action on the essential elements was key in preparing for results and achieving his own sustained, elevated performance.

John also reminds me that, at times when he was unsure he could Do what was required, his favorite coach—his wife Nancy— was always there encouraging him and reminding him of what is important.

John Peterson
OLYMPIC CHAMPION

As promised early in this chapter, we do want to share a bit more about John's mission, what he sometimes calls his "mental preparation," depending upon your willingness to engage. For John, like for the authors, he sees his ultimate mission fulfilling *1 Corinthians 10:31*[13]. If you take a look at this New Testament reference, as well as *Ephesians 2:8*, *2:9*, and *2:10*[14], you will learn more about how this mortal, John Peterson, was imminently prepared mentally, taking the focus off of his personal desires, which often cause fear, uncertainty, or pride, and putting the focus on a mission greater than himself. And, since winning his gold medal, John has dedicated his life to teaching others through Athletes-in-Action—quite another significant mission.

Regardless of whether you follow scripture, believe and apply the lesson John lived and lives: that he was made to simply become the best wrestler he could be for someone else's glory. We all want to be part of something bigger than ourselves, to experience the joy of a victory beyond what we can achieve alone, and to feel deep gratitude for the opportunity to contribute our talents and gifts.

Inspire and lead your organization toward a Vision that compels collaborative action, develops and builds the talents of others, and engages the whole organization. In your organization—today and every day—we encourage you to Do what it takes and Go for the Gold!

POISED® Key Points Summary	
People	Develop each person to their fullest capability and enable optimal utilization of their Strengths
Octane	. . . of the organization – Mission, Vision, Values (MV²) – and results driven, shaped through continuous improvement in all facets of the organization
Identify	. . . all priorities, challenges, opportunities, and metrics – to act with wise use of resources
Strategy	. . . to leverage Strengths to win for all facets of the organization, clearly communicated to all constituencies and acted upon
Engine of Profitability	. . . to fund growth supporting the Strategy to win
Do	Daily, weekly, monthly, quarterly, and annual rhythm of the business leveraging POISED® for success
POISED® Integrated Model	

7

CONCLUSION

"Continuous effort—not strength or intelligence
—is the key to unlocking our potential."
–Winston Churchill, Former Great Britain Prime Minister–

Think about the differences between an opinion, a belief, and a conviction. The differences are more than just a distinction in definitions—they illuminate human behavioral tendencies and illustrate the pathways to unlock human potential and the organizational performance capability that depends on it.

You may form an *opinion* based on an experience (yours or of someone you know), a book you read or movie you see, the news channel you watch or publications you read, social media posts you navigate, a notable speech you hear, or other sources. When you have more experiences or receive new information, you may shift your opinion—it is malleable and flexible.

When that opinion shifts to a *belief*, it gains power and begins to govern your responses and behaviors, as you attribute consequences to the belief (e.g., "because I believe in X, then Y will or will not happen"). The belief may be empowering and serve you or your team well, or it may be limiting, stalling or even preventing forward progress.

Finally, when you take deliberate and targeted action to reinforce the strength of your belief, you have demonstrated a firm and likely unwavering *conviction*. A positive conviction builds on the foundation of empowering belief and constructs a powerful, durable, and value-accruing structure.

What will you do to convert your opinions and beliefs into purpose-driven convictions?

PURPOSE

We indeed had a purpose in writing this book. We wrote for those who share a passion with us—to fulfill a purpose in leading, a purpose in leading an organization, however small or large. That purpose involves the team that they lead or of which they are an important piece. The purpose also extends into the future and the impact they can have on people's lives.

We believe strongly while you are at work, whether in one of the most competitive businesses on earth, or in a ministry serving people from your ministry-driven mission, helping people achieve higher performance and better results, in an environment inspiring them to achieve their highest potential, is a rewarding way to fulfill your purpose in leading. Making a long-lasting impact on the people and their lives is something that will outlast a job or an assignment.

Helping people achieve higher performance and better results is a rewarding way to fulfill your purpose in leading. Making a long-lasting impact on the people and their lives is something that will outlast a job or an assignment.

We are hopeful the POISED Model for organizational leadership will provide you a systematic approach with structure, priorities, and tools, that does indeed become the GPS for you and your team.

Will you and your team step up, lead the organization, and make the commitment?

COMMITMENT

If you and your organization seek sustained high performance and excellence, it is not enough to think that the POISED elements "sound like a good idea" (opinion). And your implementation will stall near (or before) the starting line if your team considers the POISED elements yet expresses limiting *beliefs* like "we have tried to be more disciplined in the past, but our culture resists change and it is too hard to stay on track" or "we would like to implement POISED, but our senior and business leaders might not be equipped or have the time to take it on."

Ask yourself:

Can I afford to stick with the status quo and keep fighting the same old battles day in, and day out?

Gaining the full benefits of the POISED Model requires *conviction*! Your leadership team must be willing to change senior and management team members, modify business systems, abandon activities that are not working, adopt new behaviors and approaches, invest financial resources, enhance training and development . . . and take many other decisive actions to enable the transformation. Develop an *empowering* belief that "when we commit to POISED, we will achieve ever-higher levels of success and value for our customers, stakeholders, and team members", then convert it into a conviction by acting diligently and with constancy of purpose.

> To earn the full benefits of the POISED Model, your leadership team must be willing to make changes . . . in senior and management team members, in business systems, in choices for investing resources, in behaviors and approaches, in training and development . . . and to take repeated, decisive actions to enable the transformation.

As you take one more look at the POISED Model, note that its clarity and simplicity underpin its power to enable organizational change. Our work with people and teams applying the POISED

Model motivates us to share it with more and more people. People have shared strong, passionate feedback. They love the emphasis on strengths and how the model motivates performance and engagement. They embrace the team-strengths concepts. They have spoken about how POISED addresses the organization's critical elements; they share how they have prepared clear, actionable Strategic Plans with specific implementation plans incorporating all elements of the organization's strengths and its needs.

Finally, we have heard that, compared to other models, the POISED Model has been clearer, more accessible, and more impactful than other approaches. We hear the time to go from lack of direction and misalignment to an organization with clarity, purpose, and accountability is far shorter than they imagined. They have implemented the POISED Model with conviction, left the status quo and old problems behind, and reaped the rewards.

As we have said, there was a purpose in committing the model we use to paper in this book. We sincerely hope that you will achieve exceptional results for your team and your organization as well.

May you impact many in your leadership role—and may *POISED® for Results* help you lead your organization to achieve sustained, elevated performance, while you add value to the lives of others and the many customers, team members, and stakeholders that they influence.

ACKNOWLEDGMENTS

Nnone of us are as smart or strong as all of us, and none of us travel our lifetime journeys on our own. We have so many to whom we owe thanks and appreciation and cannot possibly make note of the thousands of people over our lifetimes who have traveled with us as we have learned and grown as people and leaders.

While we take this opportunity to recognize some specific individuals and groups, know that we are deeply grateful to ALL who have been a part of our development and journeys. For clarity and to facilitate our recognition, we organize our thanks and extend our deep appreciation in two sections, one each for Mark and Dr. Scott, before a few final words of recognition from both of us. (Note: acknowledged people who have left this life's journey are noted below with *.)

Mark's Acknowledgments

- **My family.** I am especially thankful for my amazing wife, *Jean,* who has kept me grounded and supported me for more than 40 years. In addition, our three children who grew up globally with Jean providing so much for the family during the moves over the years: *Christina*, a successful attorney in Minnesota, *David*, who lives in New York and has a drive for impacting finance, technology, and investments, and *Mary* an HR professional in Minnesota, and their families have all been a blessing to their father (and grandfather).

My early blessing was to grow up first with *Mom* and *Dad*, and later with Dad and Stepmom, *Jean*. My mom has the gift of always showing her unwavering love to family and close friends. Dad taught us hard work. Stepmom Jean was unafraid to teach important life lessons—correct English, careful spending, etc. Learning from each of them, and their Strengths, and my four siblings who have each used their Strengths and taught through their life experiences, has been an enabler for this Learner who started life slowly, and has been allowed to accelerate ever since.

- **My teachers.** My many teachers have left deep impressions and education became a way to break out of early, undiagnosed but evident, developmental inhibitions. Two are worth specific mentions. Thank you to *Mrs. Swedensky* from Windom Elementary School in Minneapolis, who gave us books to read in class. She tested us after we read these books on our own time, and we earned five cents for reading five books—in third grade. What a motivation to finish work early and practice reading at an early age! Earning 45 cents meant I read a lot that year and experienced the first success I can remember: more books read than anyone in the third grade. Later, at the end of eighth grade, *Mrs. Zoller* challenged me to finish pre-Algebra and

Algebra in half a year after moving to Florida from Minnesota mid-year. I am grateful for all of my teachers, in school and in life, and especially those who posed audacious challenges and offered rewarding opportunities. One day, an elementary school teacher (whose name I do not remember unfortunately), happened to mention something about me being a leader. As a shy, young kid, I did not have any idea what that meant . . . but I never forgot the comment and have worked hard to live up to that ideal.

- **My teammates.** I remember the impact of learning from others in jobs well before college, from delivering newspapers in sixth and seventh grade, toiling in restaurants in eighth to twelfth grades, working at Dad's shop from an early age (as noted in Chapter 5), to taking jobs in college—so many people leading and working side-by-side. For me, work offered a place to break free from my early shyness and inhibitions over time and I am very thankful for all those who supported and believed in me. *Tim* persisted to drag me out to wrestling, thereby instilling a lifelong health focus and commitment to a workout regimen. I am thankful and deeply appreciative of so many mentors and peers who motivated and taught me. I mention a few special people knowing this leaves out so many who had a major impact as well.

  The team at GE Nuclear, led by *Dr. Steve Specker*, included *Jack Fuller*, who has become a life-long-mentor; *Mark Savoff* and *Bill Arndt*, leaders who challenged me to strive for excellence; *Carolyn Wright Shockley*, *Lee Elder*, *Lisa Mulrooney Gross* (who personally led a number of transformational organization changes), *Chuck Miyamoto*, and *Fukuda-san* of GE Power; and many others. They formed an amazing team of dedicated people intent on a positive mission. At this same business, especially earlier in my career, my behind-the-scenes mentor *George Roupe**, and my active General Manager *George Brown*, taught me in their own intense manner—both were committed to grow and develop people and the organization.

Customers who stick out the most through the amazing impact of their immense knowledge, presence, and heart include *Denny Galli*, who went from skeptical about this young leader, to treating me as a senior leader, and then presenting me with a retirement watch when I moved on to the next assignment in my early 30s; and *Mike Wallace*, who eventually led another utility (both men were senior leaders at Commonwealth Edison at the time of our work together). When Unisys CFO *Bob Brust* hired me for an unusual functional role in Europe, he enabled me to recover from a sudden, unplanned job change. I am grateful for the opportunity to learn from him and every non-Sales & Delivery organization in the business (Europe's Finance, HR, IT, Procurement, Legal, Facilities, and Procurement all reported to me) and he encouraged me as I accepted the role to head PaR Systems back in Minnesota.

Arriving at PaR, I can say I learned from and am extremely grateful for ALL of my fellow PaR team members and our ultra-interesting clients around the world. Some outstanding men and women who were part of the initial amazing team include *Matti Korpinen, Mike McKay**, *Glenn McKeag*, Barb Abrahamson, Jon Sakry*, and others. Those I must say a particular thank you to include *Albert Sturm*, who was a lifer and the heart of PaR for so long, and *Karen O'Rourke, Brad Yopp, Adam Marsh, Scott Singer*,

Rick Edger, *Don Miller* (who sold Ederer to PaR, the first of many acquisitions), *Iain Attwater, Dan Bartlett, Kallie Swartz, Wayne Skiba, Doug Westbrock, Jim Krafcik, Mary Krafcik*, and many more. Two PaR clients I will mention are *Mike Packer* of Lockheed Martin and *Gregg Stedronsky* of General Mills; I am thankful for having known them both as friends and brilliant mentors.

PaR board members like *Gary Edson* (Gary and his father *Gene* brought me to PaR from Unisys, for which I am very thankful), former Secretary of the Navy *Larry Garrett, Jack Fuller*, and *Bert Colianni* all taught me about being a good, supportive, and challenging board member. And, their alignment with the company's mission, vision, and values taught me even more. Board advisor *Matt Carter* also was very wise and helpful to the PaR board during my tenure. Today, my partners at P2G Capital—*Alex Furth, Jay Johnson, Gary Edson, David Wrightsman, Bruce Zivian*, and *Derek Vandenburgh*—all enjoy challenging one another and supporting the mission, keeping each of us on top of our game as iron sharpens iron. My partners at Partner2Learn (see partner2learn.com/our-team/) including *Dr. Scott, Paul, Jay, Dan, Tiffany, Karen*, and *Nate* all enjoy the same mission of supporting other leaders and I am grateful for the chance to continue to work with and to learn from them.

The amazing team at GIA (Grace in Action), a leadership team focused on Lutheran ministries, are all people near and dear and I would mention each one except for space limitations. Let me say that after Dr. Scott led GIA's formation, stabilization, and early growth, when we recruited *Arvid Schwartz* to the board, his experience as first CFO of Health Partners, overcoming life's obstacles, and involvement in dozens of ministries and their boards, provided so much learning, support, and encouragement to each of us and the organization. To Dr. Scott's hand-chosen successor, Pastor *Don Sutton*, we all owe a deep gratitude for showing poise and servant leadership as the organization has continued to build and to expand its ministry impact from the amazing start led by Dr. Scott.

Working with *Michelle Cambrice*, Director of the Journey School, has been an amazing learning experience for me. Michelle, along with SON Admin leader *Shannon Gostchock* and internationally experienced chef and chef trainer *Lafayette* who has volunteered serving children gourmet food for years, have been an inspiration, along with many others they are serving.

Rick Loewen has shown how unique Strengths and experiences as a police officer in difficult situations can be leveraged into coaching Pastors, all with challenging jobs leading their ministries. *John Peterson*, whose story we share in this book, has been an inspiration. *Jim Louwsma*, who had an exciting military aviation career as a pilot, was a very successful Proctor & Gamble executive, and later began coaching others, has been instrumental in demonstrating the way to stay engaged after a formal career ends; he was the one who taught me the true use of Strengths after my exposure to them once earlier in life without seeing the benefit.

Dr. Scott's Acknowledgments

- **My family.** I am incredibly thankful for my loving and talented wife of 30 years, *Shannon*; my amazing children, *Samuel*, *Tomas*, *Seth*, and *Sarai*; my supportive parents,

Barry and *Joy*; and so many other family members and extended family members. All of these amazing people have provided constant support, love, and encouragement with the belief that all things are possible through Jesus, our Lord and Savior. The appreciation I truly have for all of you cannot be stated fully in words, but I acknowledge and love you all. Thank you!

- **My teachers.** My teachers were very instrumental in my development. There are too many to identify by name, but Professor *Alan Spurgeon*, who has since passed on to heaven, was the most encouraging and talented instructor I experienced. His encouragement and always positive and uplifting messaging pushed me to be more than I ever thought I could be. One other teacher who influenced and encouraged me beyond what I ever thought possible was (and still is) *Dr. Cathy Moore*. She spurred me on to finish my Master's Degree and to pursue and to complete my Doctorate. She was and remains a positive cheerleader and encourager in all I do. I cannot thank her without also thanking her awesome husband and fellow Green Bay Packer fan, *John*. Together, they make a great team full of fun, laughter, teaching, learning, and never-ending encouragement. All of my other teachers were amazing in so many different ways. Thanks!

- **My Teammates.** *Dan* and *Tiffany Weigand* with Partner2Learn were tremendous supporters and encouragers through this whole process. These teammates help to spur me and so many others onto greatness every day. Thanks! A special thanks to *Jay Johnson* who has been a great encourager and mentor to me for so many years. I would not be where I am without him. Thanks!

It almost goes without saying, but I owe a very special thanks to *Mark Wrightsman*. He was not only my partner with this book, but in so many other aspects of my personal and professional development. Thanks!

I am grateful for all of the other teammates noted by Mark and others from the past: all of the teachers I served with over the years, all the leaders and boards I was fortunate to serve, all of the people who gave encouragement and provided leadership to help direct me throughout my life, all of the students I have ever taught (from whom I learned more than they ever learned from me), all of the families I have served who made me a part of their families . . . and so many other friends and acquaintances through the years. I value and appreciate you all. Thanks!

Acknowledgments from Mark and Dr. Scott

A few concluding words of gratitude from both of us:

- Most importantly, we acknowledge our faith in the triune God and give thanks for His work in all that we do.
- We are greatly appreciative of *Adam Cohen*, our book editor and much more, for his insightful ideas on matters large and small and his graceful edits throughout the process. Adam thoughtfully applied his organizational transformation expertise, business operations and strategic experience, book editing skills, writing and creative talents, and passion for making people's lives better to shape this book and to elevate it to new levels.
- Thank you to all of those who supported us during the writing of this book with words of encouragement we needed many times throughout this journey.

ARE YOU POISED FOR SUCCESS?

A t Partner2Learn, LLC, we believe in viewing leadership and process development through a different perspective. We take weakness out of our vocabulary and focus on strengths and partner-up opportunities. We partner with our clients using a StrengthsFirst focus that guides transformational growth in individuals, teams, and organizations. We enable an understanding and appreciation for personal strengths, and respect and acceptance of others' strengths. The result is higher employee engagement and retention rates for individuals and high-functioning teams that produce increased productivity and effectiveness.

Visit www.partner2learn.com, or email us at info@partner2learn.com.

STRENGTHSFIRST PROFESSIONAL COACHING AND SUPPORT
CULTURE BUILDING | TEAM BUILDING | EXECUTIVE COACHING
STRATEGIC PLANNING | EXECUTION

ABOUT THE AUTHORS

Scott Gostchock, Ed.D.

Top Strengths:
Relator | Achiever | Responsibility | Learner | Discipline
Communication | Individualization | Belief

Dr. Scott is the co-founder of Partner-2Learn. In his more than 26 years of educational and community service, he has served cross-cultural, inner city, and urban education settings as a teacher, administrator, and community activist. He has also served as a full-time professor of education and currently is an adjunct professor for a number of universities and colleges. These unique settings and wealth of experiences have provided a tremendous backdrop for Dr. Scott's educational presentations on CliftonStrengths (formerly StrengthsFinder), transformative leadership work, executive coaching, global leadership and more.

Dr. Scott has a Bachelor's from Dr. Martin Luther College, a Master's in Education from Brenau University; and an Ed.D. in Leadership from Nova Southeastern University.

MARK WRIGHTSMAN

Top Strengths:
Learner | Arranger | Responsibility | Achiever | Activator
Focus | Futuristic | Belief

In his more than 39-year career, Mark has worked around the globe with GE and led a privately-held automation and material handling company, helping it become a global leader as the CEO for almost 20 years. His strong focus on leading organizations toward growth and excellence grew out of experience leading six business P&Ls, as well as a 1,500-person functional organization for Unisys. Mark led organizations in Asia, Europe, and the U.S. while living in five different countries.

His transformational leadership experience building teams and drive for quality and process excellence yielded a strong, profitable growth track record throughout his career, providing a valuable asset to companies, boards, and clients he serves.

Mark has a Bachelor's in Nuclear Engineering from University of Florida and an MBA from the University of Santa Clara.

APPENDIX

1. POISED® Strategy Plan Template
2. CliftonStrengths Eight-Category Summary
3. Alignment-Engagement-Fit (AEF) Checklist
4. Driving Business Solutions (DBS) Worksheet
5. Fuel Meeting Agenda
6. Fuel Engagement Matrix
7. 9-Box Talent Management Guide
8. Rules for Productive Dialogue

POISED® STRATEGY PLAN TEMPLATE (1 OF 5)

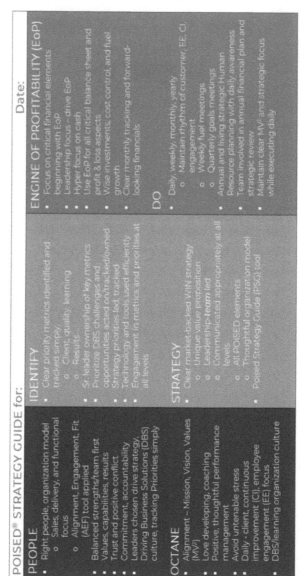

POISED® STRATEGY GUIDE for: Date:

PEOPLE
- Right people, organization model
  - Sales, delivery, and functional focus
  - Alignment, Engagement, Fit (AEF) tool applied
- Balanced strengths/team first
- Values, capabilities, results
- Trust and positive conflict
- Commitment, accountability
- Leaders chosen drive strategy
- Driving Business Solutions (DBS) culture, tracking Priorities simply

OCTANE
- Alignment – Mission, Vision, Values (MV²)
- Love developing, coaching
- Positive, thoughtful performance management
- Avoid untenable stress
- Daily - client, continuous improvement (CI), employee engagement (EE) focus
- DBS/learning organization culture

IDENTIFY
- Clear priority metrics identified and tracked simply
  - Client, quality, learning
  - Results
- Sr. leader ownership of key metrics
- Prioritize DBS challenges and opportunities acted on/tracked/owned
- Strategy priorities led, tracked
- Technology and tools used efficiently
- Engagement in metrics and priorities at all levels

STRATEGY
- Clear market-backed WIN strategy/
- Unique value proposition
- Leadership-*team led*
- Communicated appropriately at all levels
  - All POISED elements
  - Thoughtful organization model
- Poised Strategy Guide (PSG) tool

ENGINE OF PROFITABILITY (EoP)
- Focus on critical financial elements beginning with EoP
- Leadership focus – drive EoP
- Hyper focus on cash
- Use EoP for all critical balance sheet and profit & loss aspects
- Wise investments, cost control, and fuel growth
- Clear monthly tracking and forward-looking financials

DO
- Daily, weekly, monthly, yearly
  - Maintain rhythm of customer, EE, CI, engagement
    - Weekly fuel meetings
    - Quarterly goals meetings
- Annual and living strategic Human Resource planning with daily awareness
- Team involved in annual financial plan and strategic review
- Maintain clear MV² and strategic focus while executing daily

POISED® Strategy Plan Template (2 of 5)

POISED® STRATEGY GUIDE for:		Date:
MISSION: *We exist to serve...*	**VISION:** *In (5, 10, 20) years we will...*	

VALUE PROPOSITION

□ INTERNAL
- ➤ Values:
- ➤ Driving force: (Why are we here?)
- ➤ Organizational strengths: (What we do well - people, experience, operational excellence/lean, speed...)

□ MARKET/EXTERNAL
- ➤ What our customers need:
- ➤ How do we best serve customers:
- ➤ Offerings, differentiation Unique Selling Points (USP) - possibly replace offerings, other differentiation...
- ➤ Chosen market(s) and niche selection

MARKET ANALYSIS & FINANCIAL PERSPECTIVE

□ IDENTIFY/PRIORITIZE:
- ➤ Competition:
- ➤ New entrants in market:
- ➤ Economic considerations: Trends in supply chain, other partners, regional/global changes...
- ➤ Identified customer needs and trends:

□ CHALLENGES & OPPORTUNITIES (C & O)/PRIORITIZE:
1.
2.
3.
4.
5.
6.

	Current Year -3	Current Year - 2	Last Year	Current Year	Current Year + 1	Current Year + 2
Revenue						
Profit						
Key metric						

POISED® Strategy Plan Template (3 of 5)

POISED® STRATEGY GUIDE for:		Date:
MISSION: *We exist to serve...*	**VISION:** *In (5, 10, 20) years we will...*	

STRATEGY ARTICULATION

☐ STRATEGY HISTORY
☐ STRATEGY - UPDATED

➤ Organizational model/how we are leading delivery and serving clients
➤ Offerings choices (products, services,...)
➤ Emphasis in:
  1. Execution, operational excellence
  2. Sales, marketing, customer feedback
  3. Customer focus
  4. Services
  5. Products
  6. Technologies
  7. Cost
  8. Other

➤ Key strategy elements:

  A. Clear statement of strategy ("how do we best utilize our precious resources – people, time, money, leadership attention – to achieve our vision"):

  B. (Client to) Include graphics as helpful: "Five Pillars"/other models

  C. Critical business processes and needed actions/other DBS that affect our strategy implementation:

  D. Communication priorities; ensuring alignment:

POISED® STRATEGY PLAN TEMPLATE (4 OF 5)

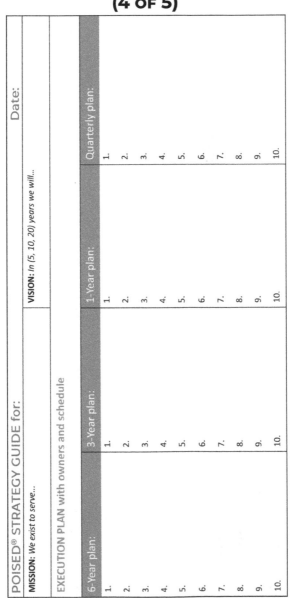

POISED® STRATEGY GUIDE for: Date:

MISSION: *We exist to serve...*   VISION: *In (5, 10, 20) years we will...*

EXECUTION PLAN with owners and schedule

6-Year plan:	3-Year plan:	1-Year plan:	Quarterly plan:
1.	1.	1.	1.
2.	2.	2.	2.
3.	3.	3.	3.
4.	4.	4.	4.
5.	5.	5.	5.
6.	6.	6.	6.
7.	7.	7.	7.
8.	8.	8.	8.
9.	9.	9.	9.
10.	10.	10.	10.

POISED® Strategy Plan Template (5 of 5)

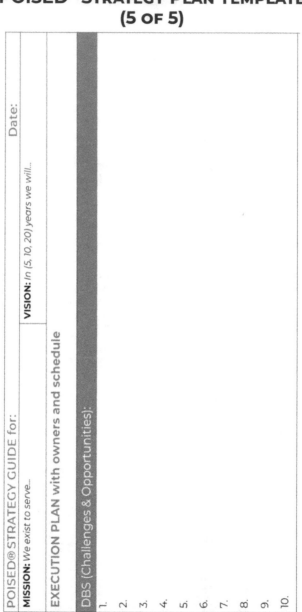

POISED® STRATEGY GUIDE for:

Date:

MISSION: *We exist to serve...*

VISION: *In (5, 10, 20) years we will...*

EXECUTION PLAN with owners and schedule

DBS (Challenges & Opportunities):

1.
2.
3.
4.
5.
6.
7.
8.
9.
10.

CliftonStrengths
Eight-Category Summary

Jim Louwsma and Dr. Mark McCloskey developed an eight-category, organizational-based CliftonStrengths Model that goes beyond the original four Gallup categories. The Strengths categories in their model are depicted below.

Traction: Strengths that get things started, like to constantly be on the go and push forward, terrific at gaining forward movement (traction), and then like to hand off to those with "Driving" strengths to finish.

Driving: These strengths are great at finishing things, like to accomplish tasks, "drive" things forward, and bring home the prize, hard charging strengths that take great joy in finishing efforts started by "Traction" strengths.

Seeing: People with the innate strength of sight, ability to see either forward or backwards in order to always inform the present and lead to the future.

Interpersonal: These strengths deal with the human touch, able to work with people and understand people, strengths in this area will always be looking for the human touch.

Lifestyle: These strengths are more flavoring in nature, they influence, "flavor" the other strengths and the use thereof, example – positivity will influence all other strengths to always be looking at the "glass as half full" – these strengths combine with others to inform decisions and actions taken.

Wild Cards: These strengths have no downside; however, for them to be used fully they must be partnered with other strengths, to learn for the sake of learning or communicate for the sake of communicating is not a use of strengths for others (SFO), when partnered with other strengths or learning new strengths for the team then full capacity is realized.

Problem Identification: The strength to see the "true" problem, sight that can see problems coming or problems being experienced, ability to cut right through the issues to the heart of the problem at hand and not the ancillary issues that might cloud true identification.

Problem Solving: The strength to solve problems and issues that exist, able to see the steps needed and intricate details that would go into a solution or plan to address any problem that might exist.

These eight categories comprise a team-based Strengths model. Grace In Action and Partner2Learn have developed further tools and leadership processes that build on CliftonStrengths and the Louwsma-McCloskey model and mesh with the POISED Model for organizational leadership.

Learn more at *partner2learn.com* and *graceinaction.com*.

ALIGNMENT-ENGAGEMENT-FIT (AEF) CHECKLIST

Every person in the organization needs to be Aligned, Engaged, and the right Fit. If any of these three areas are missing or lacking, less-than-positive results will occur. However, if all three areas are fully in place for every individual in the organization, the increased results for the team will be clearly evident.

Alignment

- Fully recognize, believe in, and carry out the organization's mission
- Understand and unequivocally accept the organization's values
- Realize and embody the vision of the organization
- Embrace and move forward with clearly stated goals and success metrics

Engagement

- Fully present and involved in organizational activities and responsibilities
- Active contributor to organizational improvement and overall quality
- Accountable to self and others for organizational success
- Live values inside and outside of the organization—community matters

Fit

- Right skills for position and duties, or ability to learn and use such skills, needed to achieve excellence
- Strengths are fully utilized in position and completes duties for the good of the organization—using those strengths for others

- Recognizing and capitalizing on partner-up opportunities with others' strengths to maximize organizational productivity and success
- Continually improving strengths, as well as and missional, emotional, and physical resiliency and health

All three AEF components are vitally important for all organizations. Alignment and Engagement are a must. If either component is missing or not firing on all cylinders, the person involved is not going to be productive. If Fit is the only issue because of training needs or other professional development, the organization must consider how much time, energy, and resources can be devoted to the individual(s) to assist them to become the right Fit.

DRIVING BUSINESS SOLUTIONS (DBS) WORKSHEET

Issues arise for every business. DBS assures we identify and discuss issues and, as a team, establish the way forward.

1. **Clarify**: Be clear on the issue. All have input, especially individuals with Problem Identification Strengths (Strategic, Ideation, Intellection). The clearly identified real issue is:

    _____

    _____

    _____

    _____

    _____

2. **Team Inputs**: Discuss important aspects related to the issue. Always keep aligned on MV^2 (Mission, Vision, and Values), identify ideas to help understand, and head toward resolution of the clarified issue (all strengths have equal emphasis in this discussion). The solution:

    _____

    _____

    _____

    _____

    _____

3. **Way Forward**: Leader facilitates the team action plan with owner(s) and timeline. All have input, especially individuals with Problem-Solving Strengths (Restorative, Input, Arranger, Analytical, Deliberative) and Traction Strengths (Focus, Activator, Command) to get everything moving.

Primary "owner" of the solution: _____

"Solved by" Goal Date: _____

Action Steps

Who	Does What (Strategy – Steps)	By When

Notes:

_____

_____

_____

_____

_____

_____

_____

_____

_____

_____

Fuel Meeting Agenda

Date: _____ **Time:** _____ (90 minutes)

Participants (Leadership Team): *Note attendance here.*

Alignment:

Review Strategic Priorities and Engine of Profitability:

Add your own here to customize.

Core Values:

Add your own here to customize.

Driving Force:

Add your own here to customize.

Leadership Expectations and Meeting Norms: Each team is fully prepared, emailing reports a minimum of 1-hour before all meetings, with a leadership/ownership mindset. Turn off devices. Start promptly. Full involvement and attention from all. *Edit and add others as desired and needed.*

StrengthsFirst for Others/Teams (5 minutes): Share a time where you used one of your strengths to help others, positively impact the team, and/or drive the organizations values and purpose/cause/passion forward. Also, if possible, share as you may have seen a teammate use their strengths in this way as a strength for others.

Identified Priority Metrics (5 minutes): Report numbers relative to client, quality, financials, and Continuous Improvement (CI) goals (metrics continuously simplified and improved). Anything warranting discussion is added to the Driving Business Solutions (DBS) section to address current business issues.

Metrics with Descriptions:

1. *Add your own here to customize.*

2. *Add your own here to customize.*
3. *Add your own here to customize.*

Goal Review (5 minutes): Review status of each leadership team goal target ("on target" or "off target"). If a goal is off target or something is standing in the way of the goal completion, immediately move to DBS section.

Owner of the goal does not have to do it all but has to own/ be accountable to report "on target" or "off target" for being completed by target date.

#	Goal	Owner	On Target	Off Target
1				
2				
3				

Vital People Updates (5 minutes): A moment where everyone in the room has an opportunity to share a concern or a celebration about anyone connected with your organization, such as employees, clients, or suppliers.

To Do List (5 minutes): Insert action items to be completed by next meeting specific to POISED goals or other important issues needing to be solved to keep all of the organization on target. You simply now ask Done or Not Done if not done, it drops down to the DBS section.

Actions/Steps Required	Resources Needed	By Date	Point Person	Outcome/Measurement

DBS Driving Business Solutions (60 minutes): Prioritize the current list. Start with the top 3 priorities. Then, complete the rest as time permits.

Priority	Issue (topic for discussion)	Solution (Who does what by when? Usually added to the new To Do List)

Conclusion (5 minutes): Tie up loose ends.

1. Review and recap New To Do list for clarity and ownership.

Actions/Steps Required	Resources Needed	By Date	Point Person	Outcome/Measurement

2. Fuel messages to team (What needs to be communicated? By/to whom, how, and when?)

3. Rate this meeting (1-10) = (How can we improve?) Rating average = ____

4. Next meeting Date and Time: _____

Attendance is required unless otherwise preapproved

Closing Comments:

Fuel Engagement Matrix

Guidelines

If you are like most leaders, you feel a bit overwhelmed because you do not have enough time to accomplish everything you want, or you work outside of your strengths. You know you need to delegate responsibilities to others who are more qualified and/or simply have strengths to use in these activities that you do not possess (partner-up opportunity).

Obviously, we cannot do only those things we love to do, but what if we could partner-up with others more effectively and efficiently to help each other and serve the organization to higher levels? It is always desirable when we, and those with whom we serve, can mutually benefit from unique strengths, interests, experiences, and passions. Follow these steps and explore the possibilities.

Process

Step 1: Define your 100%. What is your maximum energy limit? Where you do the most at your best and are not exhausted but energized? This is your 100% energy management level; do not think time management, but instead consider how to maximize your energy. Do not move to the next step without answering this question. Forward movement begins here.

Step 2: List every organizational activity you do. Review your annual, monthly, weekly, and daily schedule. Make a list of each activity, big and small. It may seem daunting, but this effort is well worth the time and is likely to save you hundreds of hours of energy every year.

Step 3: Determine if you are over maximum positive energy capacity. How much time/ energy (average per week) will it take to do everything on your list (from Step 2) to an exceptional level?

While this calculation is not easy, it is vital. If your answer exceeds your 100% positive energy management (from Step 1), it is time to partner-up.

- Peak Performance = Capacity – Interferences
- Working from your strengths takes 10%-20% effort and achieves 80%-90% results
- Conversely, working outside your strengths takes 80%-90% effort for 10%-20% results
- Working from your strengths yields four times the results with 20% the amount of energy

Step 4: Populate the Fuel Engagement Matrix. Take everything from your activity list and enter each item into the most appropriate quadrant of the Fuel Engagement Matrix (attached) which will take into account your Strengths and Experience.

Step 5: Partner-up. Learn. Teach. Ideally, stop doing (if non-essential or someone else's responsibility) or take the excess capacity items (in the lower, left quadrant of the Fuel Engagement Matrix) and partner-up with people who have more aligned strengths and passion with those items until you are within your 100% energy management capacity limit. These actions may take some time and require a plan with strategic steps (e.g., recruit and/or train others, modify position descriptions and/or organizational structure, search and find appropriate people with the best partner-up strengths, etc.). In the end, you and the organization you serve will benefit. You will have more energy and be a more productive, engaged, and successful leader.

FUEL ENGAGEMENT MATRIX

	BOTTOM - STRENGTHS	**TOP 8**
HIGH	**PARTNER-UP!** Use your experience with a partner's strengths to DO together. Add tasks and responsibilities that match your strengths, you have a lot of experience with, and you are not currently doing that you could partner-up with others to assist them in doing to bring maximum energy and results.	**DO!** Use your strengths and get it done with minimum energy. Add tasks and responsibilities that match your strengths, you have a lot of experience with, and use the least amount of energy to achieve maximum results.
LOW — EXPERIENCE	**PARTNER-UP!** Find a partner to DO it. Add tasks and responsibilities that do not match your top strengths or experience level. Partnering-up will work best to achieve maximum results and energy utilization.	**LEARN!** Gain experience to strengthen your strengths. Add tasks and responsibilities that match your strengths but require learning to gain more experience to use the least amount of energy to achieve maximum results.

Fuel Engagement Matrix

	PARTNER-UP! Use your experience with a partner's strengths to DO together.	**DO!** Use your strengths and get it done with minimum energy.
HIGH		
LOW	**PARTNER-UP!** Find a partner to DO it.	**LEARN!** Gain experience to strengthen your strengths.

EXPERIENCE

BOTTOM - STRENGTHS - TOP 8

9-BOX TALENT MANAGEMENT GUIDE

Talent Management Grid

	Low	Moderate	High
High	"Rough Diamond" Low Potential/High Performer Develop Feedback/Assignments	"Future Star" Moderate Performer/High Potential Stretch/Develop Coach/Assignments	"Consistent Star" High Performer/High Potential Stretch Mentor/Delegate Responsibility
Moderate	"Inconsistent Player" Low Performer/Moderate Potential Observe Feedback	"Key Player" Moderate Performer/Moderate Potential Develop Feedback/Coach	"Current Star" High Performer/Moderate Potential Stretch/Develop Coach/Projects
Low	"Talent Risk" Low Performance/Low Potential Bad Hire? Counsel/PIP	"Solid Professional" Moderate Performer/Low Potential Observe Feedback/Coach	"High Professional" High Performer/Low Potential Develop Assignments/Learning

Potential Assessment (vertical axis) — *Performance Assessment* (horizontal axis)

RULES FOR PRODUCTIVE DIALOGUE

DIALOGUE: a conversation between two or more people in which an exchange of ideas, views, or opinions takes place.

1. **SUSPEND ALL JUDGMENTS.** As a football fan, if you like the Vikings, you must suspend that judgment in order to truly hear the points of the Packers fan; otherwise, you only hear *arguments* back and not the *facts* stated.

2. **LISTEN: REPHRASE AND CLARIFY.** Ask people to restate what they said ("did I hear you say X?"); then they can respond ("what I meant to say was Y") and you can achieve clarity.

3. **IDENTIFY ASSUMPTIONS.** Make sure the real issues are the real issues based upon facts, truth, and reality and not what you think it *might* or *should* be.

4. **USE INQUIRY.** Question and identify question(s) that need to be answered. Now ask questions and dig deep to make sure all is accurate; you may need to go backwards to re-identify issues and discussion points, but digging deep into the issues here through questions will makes sure you discuss and work towards a solution of the true problem—and really stop the bleeding—and do not just address symptoms or put a band-aid on a severed artery.

5. **REFLECT.** Very rarely does a decision need to be made "on the spot"; take time to reflect and use your critical thinking before making the final decision/judgment.

SUGGESTED READING

Bennett, William J. 2018. Tried by Fire: The Story of Christianity's First Thousand Years. Nashville, TN: Thomas Nelson.

Bonhoeffer, Dietrich. 2020. The Cost of Discipleship. Grand Rapids, MI: Reformed Church Publications.

Bossidy, Lawrence and Ram Charan. 2002. Execution: The Discipline of Getting Things Done. New York, NY: Random House.

Charan, Ram. 2013. Boards That Deliver: Advancing Corporate Governance From Compliance to Competitive Advantage. San Francisco, CA: Jossey-Bass.

Coffey, Wayne. 2005. The Boys of Winter: The Untold Story of a Coach, a Dream, and the 1980 U.S. Olympic Hockey Team. New York, NY: Crown Publishing Group.

Collins, Jim and Morten Hansen. 2011. Great by Choice. New York, NY: HarperCollins Publishers.

Collins, Jim. 2001. Good to Great. London, England: Random House Business Books.

Collins, Jim. 2002. Built to Last. 3rd ed. New York, NY: HarperCollins Publishers.

Collins, Jim. 2009. How the Mighty Fall. New York, NY: Harper-Collins Publishers.

Covey, Stephen R. 2004. The 7 Habits of Highly Effective People. New York, NY: Free Press.

Covey, Stephen R. 1994. First Things First. New York, NY: Fireside.

Deming, W. Edwards. 1990. Out of the Crisis: Quality, Productivity and Competitive Position. Cambridge, MA: Cambridge University Press.

Goldratt, Eliyahu M. and Jeff Cox. 1992. The Goal. 2nd ed., Revised. Great Barrington, MA: North River Press.

Greenleaf, Robert K. 1977. Servant Leadership, A Journey into the Nature of Legitimate Power & Greatness. Mahwah, NJ: Paulist Press.

Grove, Andrew S. 2013. Only the Paranoid Survive: How to Exploit the Crisis Points That Challenge Every Company. New York, NY: Crown Business.

Imai, Masaaki. 1986. Kaizen: The Key to Japan's Competitive Success. Singapore: McGraw-Hill.

International Bible Society. 1999. Holy Bible: New International Edition. Colorado Springs, CO: International Bible Society.

Jennings, Jason. 2012. Think Big, Act Small. New York, NY: Penguin Random House.

Kaplan, Robert S. and David P. Norton. 2009. The Balanced Scorecard: Translating Strategy Into Action. Boston, MA: Harvard Business School.

Kaplan, Robert S. and David P. Norton. 2001. The Strategy-Focused Organization: How Balance Scorecard Companies Thrive in the New Business Environment. Boston, MA: Harvard Business School.

Khalso, Mahan, Stephen R Covey, and Randy Illig. 2014. Let's Get Real or Let's Not Play: Transforming the Buyer/Seller Relationship. New York, NY: Portfolio.

Kidder, Tracy. 2003. Mountains Beyond Mountains. New York, NY: Random House.

Kouzes, James M., and Barry Z. Posner. 2017. The Leadership Challenge. 6th ed. New York, NY: John Wiley & Sons.

Lane, Bill. 2007. Jacked Up: The Inside Story of How Jack Welch Talked GE into Becoming the World's Greatest Company. New York, NY: McGraw-Hill.

Lencioni, Patrick. 2002. The Five Dysfunctions of a Team: A Leadership Fable. San Francisco, CA: Jossey-Bass.

Liker, Jeffrey K. 2004. The Toyota Way. New York, NY: McGraw-Hill.

Marshall, Peter and David Manuel. 2009. The Light and The Glory: 1492-1793. Grand Rapids, MI: Revell.

Maxwell, John C. 1993. Developing the Leader Within You. Nashville, TN: Thomas Nelson.

McCloskey, Mark, Jim Louwsma, and Dave Aeilts. 2014. The Art of Virtue-Based Transformational Leadership: Building Strong Businesses, Organizations and Families. Bloomington, MN: The Wordsmith.

Pattanaik, Devdutt. 2015. Business Sutra: A Very Indian Approach to Management. New Delhi, India: Aleph Book Company.

Senge, Peter. 2006. The Fifth Discipline: The Art and Practice of the Learning Organization. London, England, U.K.: Random House Books.

Slater, Robert. 1993. The New GE: How Jack Welch Revived an American Institution. Homewood, IL: Business One.

Slater, Robert. 1994. Get Better or Get Beaten: Leadership Secrets of Jack Welch. Burr Ridge, IL: Irwin Professional Publishing.

Thrall, Bill, Bruce McNicol, and Ken McElrath. 1999. The Ascent of a Leader: How Ordinary Relationships Develop Extraordinary Character and Influence. San Francisco, CA: Jossey-Bass Publishers.

Turner, Dee Ann. 2019. Bet on Talent: How to Create a Remarkable Culture That Wins the Hearts of Customers. Grand Rapids, MI: Baker Books.

Vroom, Victor Harold and Arthur G. Jago. 1988. The New Leadership: Managing Participation in Organizations. Englewood Cliffs, NJ: Prentice Hall.

White, John. 1986. Excellence in Leadership: Reaching Goals With Prayer, Courage & Determination. Downers Grove, IL: InterVarsity Press.

Wickman, Gino. 2012. Traction: Get a Grip on Your Business. New York, NY: BenBella Books.

CITATIONS

1   CliftonStrengths, originally Gallup's StrengthsFinder, entails an online assessment that produces a clear report on an individual's Strengths that explains why the individual performs certain activities so well. Visit Gallup's website at gallup.com/cliftonstrengths for more information.

2   Collins, Jim. 2001. Good to Great. London, England: Random House Business Books.

3   Lencioni, Patrick. 2002. The Five Dysfunctions of a Team: A Leadership Fable. San Francisco, CA: Jossey-Bass.

4   Turner, Dee Ann. 2019. Bet on Talent: How to Create a Remarkable Culture That Wins the Hearts of Customers. Grand Rapids, MI: Baker Books.

5   Coffey, Wayne. 2005. The Boys of Winter: The Untold Story of a Coach, a Dream, and the 1980 U.S. Olympic Hockey Team. New York, NY: Crown Publishing Group.

6   Senge, Peter. 2006. The Fifth Discipline: The Art and Practice of the Learning Organization. London, England, U.K.: Random House Books.

7   Covey, Stephen R. 1994. First Things First. New York, NY: Fireside.

8   Marshall, Peter and David Manuel. 2009. The Light and The Glory: 1492-1793. Grand Rapids, MI: Revell. 152-153.

9   Marshall, Peter and David Manuel. 2009. The Light and The Glory: 1492-1793. Grand Rapids, MI: Revell. 152-153.

10 International Bible Society. 1999. Holy Bible: New International Edition. Colorado Springs, CO: International Bible Society.

11 Advanced Print Technologies. "Harris M300M 6-Color Heatset Web Offset Printing Press." YouTube Video. May 1, 2018. https://youtu.be/q2oBCQo4bcU/. Listen for 30 seconds and keep that never-ending cadence in mind as your Engine of Profitability (EoP) focus.

12 Thrall, Bill, Bruce McNicol, and Ken McElrath. 1999. The Ascent of a Leader: How Ordinary Relationships Develop Extraordinary Character and Influence. San Francisco, CA: Jossey-Bass Publishers.

13 International Bible Society. 1999. Holy Bible: New International Edition. Colorado Springs, CO: International Bible Society.

14 International Bible Society. 1999. Holy Bible: New International Edition. Colorado Springs, CO: International Bible Society.

A free ebook edition is available with the purchase of this book.

To claim your free ebook edition:

1. Visit MorganJamesBOGO.com
2. Sign your name CLEARLY in the space
3. Complete the form and submit a photo of the entire copyright page
4. You or your friend can download the ebook to your preferred device

Print & Digital Together Forever.

Snap a photo

Free ebook

Read anywhere